ON
STUDYING SINGING

by SERGIUS KAGEN

DOVER PUBLICATIONS, INC.
NEW YORK

Published in Canada by General Publishing Company, Ltd., 30 Lesmill Road, Don Mills, Toronto, Ontario.
Published in the United Kingdom by Constable and Company, Ltd., 10 Orange Street, London WC 2.

This Dover edition, first published in 1960, is an unabridged and unaltered republication of the work originally published by Rinehart & Company, Inc. in 1950.

Standard Book Number: 486-20622-X
Library of Congress Catalog Card Number: 61-431

Manufactured in the United States of America
Dover Publications, Inc.
180 Varick Street
New York, N. Y. 10014

Preface

Anyone who has had the opportunity to observe and work with a number of young people studying singing no doubt knows the singular confusion and the extraordinarily haphazard manner in which most of them seem to approach their task.

It seemed to me that a short book which would discuss the nature of the general problems of studying singing, and some ways of procedure and approach which might assist the student in solving such general problems, would in turn help the student to help himself.

This little book deals primarily with the following matters: the nature of the minimal natural equipment which this writer considers indispensable to the serious study of singing; the scope and purpose of the various branches of studies involved in studying singing (such as music, languages, vocal technic, etc.); and, finally, the basic procedures a student may adopt in trying to master any of these subjects.

It is not intended to teach the student how to sing; no book could possibly do this. Its main purpose is to help him find a way to study singing intelligently.

Table of Contents

ON STUDYING SINGING

I. The Musical Ear and the Natural Voice

Singing is essentially a very simple and normal activity. Anyone who can carry a tune and is capable of producing pleasing sounds with his voice can sing. The study of singing is often considered a formidable and exacting undertaking that requires years of unremitting toil. This attitude toward the study of singing is warranted only if it is applied to those who have no natural aptitude nor talent. For those who do possess enough natural aptitude and talent, the study of singing can be an extraordinarily simple process. The pursuit of perfection in singing and the study of all the related subjects necessary for perfection can never cease; however, the fundamentals of singing necessary for professional activity are so simple that they can sometimes be acquired in a surprisingly short time, provided, of course, one is sufficiently well endowed.

Practically every normal person can sing after a fashion. One does not even necessarily have to study singing or music to be able to do so. Nearly every person who can sing after a fashion can improve his singing by proper study to some certain limited degree. "Limited degree" is used here advisedly. It matters little how ardently one may desire to learn to sing beautifully or how long and strenuously one may be willing to study to attain this goal. If one's natural endowment hap-

3

pens to be inadequate, no amount of wishing or working will change it any more successfully than wishing or working will change the color of one's eyes. Not many people possess enough natural endowment to hope to go beyond this limited degree of improvement. Of these few, only a handful may be fortunate enough to possess, at least to some degree, most of the mental, personal and physical qualifications indispensable to those who hope to become professional singers. I should like to define a professional singer rather narrowly as one whose income is derived from singing for other people.

In my experience, I have become aware of the fact that too many young people who hope to become professional singers believe too much in and expect too much from the processes of study.

Study in the performing arts is indispensable and all-important if its purpose is to bring under control and thus improve and put to use certain faculties which the student already possesses. Study as such, however, cannot be expected to endow the student with faculties he may not possess by nature. Study can make a gifted person use his gifts more efficiently—it cannot make an ungifted person less ungifted. In the performing arts, abundant natural endowment is the only foundation upon which any hope for future professional activity can be based. It seems reasonable to assume then that the amount, quality and intensity of study can produce results only in direct ratio to the amount of natural aptitude and talent a student may possess.

All this is not meant to imply that unless one has an extraordinary gift one should not study singing. On the contrary, I believe that any and every person will undoubtedly benefit and derive great pleasure from the study of the fundamentals of this art. However, being able to sing after a fashion offers no basis for much hope for a professional future.

4

It is a regrettable fact that the number of those who admit to be amateur singers is growing steadily smaller while the number of those who pretend to be professionals is growing steadily larger. It seems as though practically everyone who ever took a few lessons in singing has the hope to become a professional. These hopes are often based on the singular idea that intensive and expensive study will furnish one with the faculties nature may have denied him.

It may safely be said that in no branch of human endeavor is the lack of natural endowment more painfully apparent than it is in the arts. It may further be said that in no branch of the arts is a trained but ungifted person as pitifully inadequate as he is in music. One could add that in no branch of music is the possession of superior natural endowment more indispensable than it is in singing.

Every person who desires to study singing for the purpose of making it his profession ought to do his very utmost to discover how much natural endowment he may possess before he considers such a step seriously. Singing for one's own pleasure demands only the desire to sing; singing for other people's pleasure demands certain standards of excellence. Professional singing, however, is an entirely different undertaking. To begin with, it is a competitive activity. The standards of excellence are as high as the greatest singers of the generation may happen to set them. Nothing but an unusual natural gift plus the most exacting control of it attained through the proper study can hope to compete under such circumstances.

We have no scale of measurements which would enable us to ascertain the presence and the quality of talent. Talent seems to be the sum total of so many intangibles that it defies definition. We still know too little about ourselves even to attempt a profitable discussion of such intangibles. It has been aptly said that talent is conspicuous by its absence; but in singing,

5

perhaps much more easily than in any other branch of the performing arts, one may describe certain natural aptitudes, the possession of which would seem indispensable to any vocal student who wishes to acquire even the very lowest form of professional competence. In discussing such aptitudes, we need not even touch on the subject of talent. The possession of such aptitudes may or may not go together with the possession of a talent. In the performing arts, however, any practical use of a talent seems unthinkable when most of such aptitudes are absent.

The terms "natural aptitude," "endowment," "ability" or "equipment" are used here to designate certain mental and physical traits necessary for singing which the individual possesses before he begins to study.

The origin of such traits is of little importance in so far as this particular discussion is concerned. We have as yet no means to establish precisely how such traits originate. They may be inherited, they may be the result of environmental conditions or they may have been developed in infancy or early childhood by the individual himself. Countless other factors are no doubt involved in producing such natural fitness for any art.

The fact, however, that some individuals seem to possess a natural fitness for singing while others do not is incontrovertible, whatever the reasons for it may be.

In my experience, I have encountered many serious-minded vocal students who seemed to lack most of the aptitude vitally necessary for their future profession. Most of these students hoped to acquire such aptitudes by study. It would seem, therefore, helpful to discuss the nature of such aptitudes. Most people recognize the fact that not everyone can become a singer, but too many voice students seem to lose this platitudinous, common-sense point of view when it is their own ability that is concerned. Interpreting the deeply spiritual maxim that faith can move mountains to mean that determination and hard work can do likewise, many students set out in quest of the impossible. Often they even taken pride in embarking upon and persevering in this quixotic undertaking. A similar confusion seems to affect, to some degree, all branches of study. The hitch-your-wagon-to-a-star attitude challenges the indispensability of natural endowment, substituting for it the splendid virtues of earnestness and diligence. "No one complains if his undersized son with awkward legs does not become a football hero. Some . . . however seem to demand the intellectual equivalent of such a miracle," says Dr. James Bryant Conant, President of Harvard University, in his remarkable article, "Education for a Classless Society."

If we consider the nature of an aptitude, we could define it as a form of coordination which is apparently based upon the presence of certain physical and mental characteristics. Theoretically it may seem not impossible to acquire such coordination by guided effort or study; practically the possibility of acquiring aptitudes necessary for singing professionally must be considered in relation to the amount of time such an undertaking would require. We know that some people possess most or all of such necessary aptitudes before they begin to study. Should those who lack any or most of such aptitudes compete with those who do possess them? Should they compete in a profession which requires the continuous use of these very aptitudes? A student would not be able to accomplish anything as a singer by trying to acquire laboriously, over long periods of years, such necessary basic coordination; for the actual study of singing can only begin once this basic coordination is present.

To my knowledge, attempts to acquire forcibly any of such basic coordination which the vocal student does not naturally possess to some degree, seldom, if ever, are successful. Under such circumstances, mild neurotic counterpatterns usually set in. They seem to nullify the efficient use of all that the student may have learned. In public performance, the entire laboriously constructed edifice of such an artificially induced coordination invariably collapses revealing the natural ineptitude for singing in its pitiable nakedness. I see nothing desirable or commendable in such attempts at a violent conquest of self. There is nothing noble, self-abnegatory or heroic in attempting to disregard one's natural limitations. The contention that man is perfectible and that he should be encouraged to overcome his inadequacies has little, if any, bearing upon the study of singing for professional purposes. To work and study for years, to subject oneself to veritable torture in the hope of one day acquiring the very basic qualifications for singing professionally, qualifications which the properly endowed person possesses before he begins to study, does seem ill-advised, futile and pitiable.

The very first prerequisite which a student with professional ambition must possess is a specific variety of a very keen musical ear. The entire process of singing rests upon this. This specific variety of musical ear is the cornerstone of singing. Without it everything else is useless.

The kind of musical ear necessary for a singer can be best defined as a natural ability to imagine accurately (that is, to hear mentally) pitches or musical sounds and to reproduce the imagined pitches by whistling, humming or singing. A person may have a good ability to imagine pitches without having the complementary coordination which would enable him to reproduce them accurately with his own sound-producing apparatus. Not infrequently one encounters such a lack of complementary coordination even among musicians. Those, however, who lack this complementary coordination will, in my opinion, have too difficult a time in trying to learn how to sing to make it worth their while. The possession of this ability has nothing to do with one's sincere love for music, or with the strength of one's emotional reaction to music. One could even venture to say that it has nothing to do with musical talent. Likewise, it has nothing to do with the knowledge of musical notation, of theory of music, of vocal technic or of the technic of a musical instrument.

One must remember that, in the history of singing, one can find a great many authenticated examples of excellent singers who did not even know the elements of musical notation. Possessing naturally an excellent musical ear and an excellent coordination between the ear and the voice, such singers could learn, memorize and perform most intricate series of pitch patterns by simply listening to some one else play these pitch patterns for them on a musical instrument.

If the ability to imagine and reproduce pitches were synonymous with the knowledge of musical notation and related matters, such a phenomenon would be inexplicable and miraculous. Everyone, however, at one time or another has, no doubt, come in contact with all kinds of "non-musical" people of most diverse cultural and educational backgrounds who, knowing nothing of musical notation, are able to sing nicely on pitch. Sometimes they can also "harmonize" with others—that is, devise and sing "by ear" the alto, tenor or bass part to a tune. The fact that such people exist in rather large numbers would seem to demonstrate that a good ability to imagine and reproduce pitches is not inherently connected with any formal knowledge of music.

The ability to imagine and reproduce pitches is a coordinatory pattern which can be greatly developed once it is present, but can hardly be acquired by a more or less mature person to any serviceable degree for any practical, profes-

9

sional purpose. The development of this ability is a discipline called ear training. Its purpose lies in making a student more aware of the pitch and rhythm differences he already hears, even though he may not know their names or the written symbols representing them. Ear training quickens a student's reaction to pitches and rhythms through specially devised exercises. It also coordinates his natural pitch and rhythm discrimination with his eye (musical notation, reading music), and with the names of pitches, pitch relations and pitch combinations and rhythms (musical nomenclature). This type of training should ideally continue until the student's reactions to the written and verbal symbols representing pitches, pitch combinations and rhythms, as well as to pitches and rhythms he hears played or sung, become instantaneous, accurate and interchangeable. All this training, however, at least in so far as I have been able to ascertain, has little effect upon a more or less mature person who has a poor natural ear. If anything, it often tends to make him self-conscious and even less able to imagine and reproduce the most simple pitch and rhythm progressions which he might have been able to do before.

The difference between musical ear and ear training is little known and much less appreciated among vocal students than it ought to be. Natural aptitude and a system of study devised to improve efficiency of its control and operation complement each other; but ear training cannot be expected to create a musical ear, that is, in practice. Theoretically, this may not be impossible, especially if such training is begun at a very early age, practically in childhood. Vocal students with poor natural ear, however, often expect the study of ear training, theory and some musical instrument to produce a radical change in their ability to imagine and reproduce pitches. I suppose if they spent some twenty years at it at the rate of three or four hours a day with a most angelically patient teacher, they might acquire some of the basic coordination which a person with a good musical ear already has latently before he begins to study.

How is one to establish if he has or has not a good musical ear? Although the ability to read music accurately is, in a singer, a most certain indication of the possession of a musical ear, the inability to read music efficiently may not in the least indicate its absence. Reading music is a process by which symbols indicating pitches and rhythms are translated into equivalent sounds. It is unthinkable that this can be done accurately by a singer who lacks the necessary natural aptitude. However, to be able to do so requires specialized training. The contention that a singer who is unable to read music must lack a natural ear is not any more logical than the contention that an unlettered person must lack the faculty of speech.

There are many ways to test one's musical ear other than the test of reading which presupposes not only the possession of a natural ability, but the full trained control of such ability. For instance: Can you reproduce accurately, by whistling, singing or humming, a pitch or a series of pitches sung or played for you? If you cannot do this with any degree of ease, the chances are that you do not possess the necessary natural ability. If you can do this easily, can you reproduce accurately a tune or a fraction of a tune sung or played for you? If so, how intricate and how long a tune can you reproduce accurately and after how many hearings? Can you devise and sing, hum or whistle a second part to a tune you know while this tune is being sung or played? One of the most thorough and fair tests of this kind would be to study elementary musical notation (not theory) and elementary sight singing (not dictation) for a period of some six months. If by the end of such period one's ability to imagine and reproduce pitches remains unimproved it would seem reasonable to assume that one possesses little, if any, of this ability. Innumerable effective tests of this nature could be devised by anyone who wishes to face squarely the issue of whether his ear is good enough for the purposes of professional singing or not. It seems to me, however, that many vocal students decline to face this issue altogether. The reason for this may lie in the extraordinary confusion of terms and concepts which seems to affect much of our thinking where singing is concerned. The lack of differentiation between acquirable skills and natural aptitudes makes many a definition of musicianship and musicality vague and misleading.

Many a person with an excellent natural ear and a good natural voice, for instance, never dared to venture into the field of singing, for which he might have been splendidly equipped, because after a few desultory ill-directed and unsuccessful attempts at learning musical theory and nomenclature, he concluded that he was simply not "musical."

Many more seem to suffer from the delusion that they are musically sufficiently well equipped to become professional singers simply because they enjoy music and have learned to name notes, chords and intervals on the printed page. That merely indicates familiarity with musical notation and nomenclature. The distinction between being able to *hear* pitches, intervals and chords, and only being able to *identify* the *printed signs* indicating pitches, intervals and chords is enormous.

If a singer hears a piece of music and is able to write it down, it is an accomplishment denoting excellent musical ear and a mind which has been excellently trained. If a singer looks at a piece of music and is able to sing, hum or whistle any of its parts without being too certain of the nomenclature, it denotes an equally good ear but a mind not trained to the same degree of excellence. But if a singer looks at a piece of music and is unable to prove that he can imagine and reproduce the sound of it, even though he can identify all the printed symbols representing pitches, intervals, chords and modulations, it merely proves that he has a trained mind.

Peculiarly enough, many people seem to conclude that the ability to identify what one sees is synonymous with the ability to identify what one hears. Yet the knowledge that two dots separated by a certain number of spaces on ruled paper represent the interval of a fifth does not, in any way, insure the ability to imagine what such an interval sounds like. Knowledge of musical nomenclature is valuable provided it is based on aural perception first and on visual perception in a complementary fashion. Knowledge of musical nomenclature, however, based primarily on visual perception is almost useless, especially for a singer. This knowledge cannot, under any circumstances, serve as a substitute for a natural ability to imagine or mentally hear pitches.

Therefore, advisedly I put the possession of a good musical ear, or the ability to imagine and reproduce pitches, as the very first prerequisite necessary for a professional singer, even above the possession of a pleasant voice. The reason for this lies in the very nature of the human sound-producing mechanism. We all know that vocal cords contract in a certain fashion and that the exhaled air passing through them makes them vibrate. This action produces sound. By the aid of the tongue, lips and other numerous factors, this sound is shaped into word, pitch, grunt or an imitation of a rooster, according to our desire. An automatic coordination between the conception of a desired sound and its production definitely exists, barring pathological abnormalities within the sound-producing mechanism of a human being. The universality of speech could not otherwise be explained, since we know that of the people who learn to speak, over 99.99% have no knowledge whatsoever of the mechanical aspects of their sound-producing apparatus and its workings. Notwithstanding this lack of knowledge, they learn to produce the sounds they wish to produce. They learn to speak "by ear," that is, by first hearing, then imagining and then reproducing sound patterns. Deaf mutes offer an excellent illustration of the fact that a normal person controls his sound-producing mechanism by imagining the sound and thus unconsciously setting in motion the muscular contractions necessary for its production, and not by executing a series of planned muscular contractions. It has been demonstrated that deaf mutes are mute not because their sound-producing apparatus is defective, but because they were deaf at birth or had been deafened in early infancy. Unable to hear, they cannot learn to imagine sounds and, therefore, cannot learn to produce them. To learn to approximate even minimally effective speech sounds, they must be taught laboriously, by rote, the muscular contractions involved in their production. It seems obvious that a series of muscular contractions necessary for the production of a sound can hardly be set in motion with any degree of ease and efficiency if the person desirous of producing this sound cannot summon a clear image of it in his own mind. Most of us seem to possess the ability to imagine speech sounds adequately for all practical purposes, but the ability to imagine musical sounds or pitches seems to be much less common.

Again, theoretically it may not be impossible to acquire such ability. Practically, however, it would seem rather ill-advised to try to become a professional singer if such an ability is only present in a minimal degree, since pitch production is one of the cardinal prerequisites of music and thus of singing. An instrumentalist can press down a key, a valve or a string in a specified manner and the action will automatically produce the desired pitch on a keyboard instrument or its very near approximation on string or most wind instruments. Production of a pitch could thus be reduced, in its essentials, to digital efficiency and, unfortunately, often it is no more than just that. Because of the nature of their instruments, the keyboard instrumentalist possessing only an inferior musical ear may attain a surprising degree of pitch-producing efficiency (providing his instrument is well tuned). Wind and string players need a much better musical ear than a keyboard instrumentalist to attain even approximately the same degree of efficiency in producing accurate pitches. No digital or other conscious muscular activity can, however, be substituted for a correct conception of a pitch image where the human voice is concerned. A singer has no keys, valves or strings which he could learn to manipulate accurately enough even to approximate correct pitches. In view of all this, it seems logical to assume that the singer, above all musicians, needs most the ability to imagine pitch. Without it, he cannot begin to make music with his sound-producing apparatus even if this apparatus is capable of emitting resonant and agreeable tones.

Put simply, the whole matter of musical ear necessary for a singer may be formulated as the ability to "carry a tune" effortlessly and accurately. This is the first prerequisite of singing. The more naturally efficient this ability is, the better the chance one has to become a professional singer. This ability has to be present to some very marked degree before study, and those who hope to acquire it by study are bound for disappointment.

It is advisedly that I omit a discussion of rhythm in this chapter. The ability to produce sound in accordance with some designated rhythmic pattern can, according to all available evidence, be acquired by any normal person.

The second prerequisite which a prospective professional singer must possess is a natural singing voice. In discussing this the following must be considered at the outset: first, the general concept of what constitutes a natural singing voice is largely subject to personal tastes; second, the human voice is capable of improvement; and third, the degree to which one believes a voice can be improved has an enormous influence on one's idea of what a natural singing voice must be able to do in its untrained state.

We may speak more or less categorically of what a natural musical ear is, or, at least is not, and predict with some degree of certainty to what extent it may be developed by study. But the discussion of what a natural singing voice is or is not cannot possibly be as clear cut. Too great a portion of such a discussion would be concerned with matters of personal tastes, of cultural backgrounds and of personal beliefs.

It is clear that the possession of an excellent natural singing voice is somewhat less imperative than the possession of a natural musical ear. A person with an obviously poor natural musical ear and an obviously good singing voice cannot have much hope, as we have demonstrated, in being successfully trained to become an efficient singer; a person with an excellent ear and a mediocre voice, may, however, under certain circumstances, develop into an exceptionally valuable singer.

The whole subject of whether an ordinary speaking voice may be transformed into a singing voice or how such a transformation is to be induced rests on aesthetics and beliefs placed in the efficacy of certain "voice building" or "voice developing" methods. Many of such methods seem diametrically opposed to one another. Many adherents of any of such methods claim that only their "method" offers the vocal student a way to attain the maximum and optimum of his potentialities. If one is acquainted with a variety of such methods, one loses hope in the possibility of discussing the subject rationally. Beliefs in some particular form of voice development could be placed in the same category as religious and political beliefs.

It would seem fair, therefore, to conduct the discussion on a more personal basis. A natural singing voice must, in my opinion, have quality, or at least be capable of producing pleasing sounds before it is trained. What constitutes a pleasing sound is, of course, a matter in which no objective standards seem possible at present. We all agree, however, that some voices seem to produce unpleasing sounds. I should venture to suggest that a person who is unable to produce what he, or those in whose judgment he has the utmost confidence, consider pleasing sounds with his voice before studying would do best not to contemplate professional singing. I know that many will immediately object, saying that one may be taught how to produce pleasing sounds. Even though I agree with this to some extent, I do not believe that everyone can be taught how to produce pleasing sounds. It does not seem unreasonable to suppose that a student who can produce pleasing sounds naturally has a much better chance of becoming a professional singer than one who is, to begin with, handicapped with a voice which produces unpleasing sounds.

I should further venture to suggest that a natural voice must be capable of producing pleasing sounds of a certain volume, in other words, loud enough to be heard by some few hundred people assembled in one place for that purpose. Again, I do not dispute the fact that volume can be developed to some degree. I do not see, however, how this admission would invalidate my contention that a prospective professional singer ought to possess a practicably audible voice.

It hardly seems unreasonable to expect a future professional singer to possess at least a pitch range of an octave and a half

17

before he begins to study. Again, I must insist that I am fully cognizant of the claim that range can develop with time and practice.

Next, I should expect a natural singing voice to be able to sustain a note without trembling. Some tremolos are curable; some, however, seem to persist no matter what is done to correct them. It surely does not seem unreasonable to warn a prospective professional singer of the possibility that this affliction may not be cured by proper study.

In other words, my entire attitude concerning the natural singing voice in its untrained state can be summed up as follows: if a person is not able to produce, before training, at least some sounds which approach in quality and steadiness (not necessarily volume) the sounds one expects from a professional singer, possessing a similar type of voice whose singing one happens to admire, the chances are that this person has an inadequate natural singing voice.

One of the best ways to satisfy one's curiosity on this subject is to make several records. Sing a simple tune you know well, preferably unaccompanied. If the tune is accurately on pitch throughout, and if the quality of the voice is not displeasing, the sustained tone not quavering, and if one can encompass at least one octave without straining, it would seem not unreasonable to assume that there is some minimal indication of both ear and voice being present.

I know that it is very difficult to be dispassionate and honest with oneself in matters which concern one's own abilities. I must repeat that I am fully aware of the fact that the human voice is capable of development, but I have also seen what fatal mistakes can be committed when an "I have not studied long enough—I will improve with study and work" attitude is applied to the very fundamental requirements of singing.

It should be borne in mind that the possession of a *natural* singing voice is not due solely to the purely physical, structural characteristics of one's sound-producing apparatus. A very complex combination of emotional and intellectual factors, of coordinatory patterns possibly established very early in life, and of structural, physiological factors apparently results in the possession of such a singing voice.

This combination is so very complex and as yet so unexplored that, again, the only reasonable attitude toward the problem seems to be a purely practical one. Those who for one reason or another do not possess this complex combination of mental and physical traits should not place too much hope in the processes of study to acquire it, especially if this study is pursued for professional purposes.

It should be clearly understood that all this does not necessarily apply to the study of singing for one's own pleasure. I sincerely believe that everyone who really wishes to study singing just because it pleases him to do so, should do so, whether he has any natural ability or not. On the other hand, I do not believe that people ought to be encouraged to spend the most productive years of their lives, a great deal of money they often can ill afford, and untold effort in training for a profession which they may wish to enter but for which they may be naturally unfitted.

One could add to these two cardinal tangible requirements (musical ear and a natural voice) two others of a relatively less imperative nature: excellent health and good appearance. Of these two, perhaps, of greater importance is excellent health. People afflicted with heart disease, asthma, chronic irritations of the respiratory tract and other diseases which may have a direct bearing upon the use of their sound-producing apparatus, should consider the fact that a professional singer performs not on days which suit him, but on whatever date he happens to be engaged to perform.

As for good appearance, it is, of course, becoming more and more important all the time with moving pictures and television gradually offering more opportunities for singers.

These, then, are the four prerequisites, two of them of cardinal importance, without which no student may hope to become a professional singer. They are sufficiently tangible to be discussed rationally and sufficiently important, in my opinion, to be taken seriously. The possession of all of these prerequisites may not, however, in itself, make one an acceptable singer. Much more than this is needed. One must take into consideration such things as personality, imagination, poise, emotional power, power of projection, dramatic ability, poetic sensitivity, love for singing, character, ability to profit by criticism, patience, courage, intelligence, and last, but by no means least, a deeply rooted, innate musicality which enables a fine singer to do mysterious things with a series of pitches and rhythms which is sometimes inadequately called phrasing. All these qualities defy concise description. All, and probably many more, go into the making of talent. Without talent, the possession of aptitudes produces nothing noteworthy, but the possession of all these intangible traits cannot, in itself, make a singer either unless the two first prerequisites are not only present, but present to an exceptional degree.

II. The Study of General Musicianship

The study of singing could be divided into four primary and several secondary subjects. It is my purpose to discuss in detail only the primary subjects since the secondary subjects do not seem to present any particularly complex problem to most students.

The primary and secondary subjects which constitute the study of singing could be defined as follows:

Primary subjects:

1—Study of pitches, rhythms, their combinations and relationships; this includes ear training (sight singing and dictation) and theory (harmony, counterpoint, form, etc.) and could be called general musicianship.

2—Study of speech and allied subjects; this includes general phonetics, pronunciation, enunciation, languages and their grammar, poetry and its recitation. It includes, therefore, some fundamental principles of acting.

3—Study of matters pertaining to the efficient control of the operation of one's sound-producing mechanism (tone production, voice placement or vocal technic) and in some instances of ways and means to improve and develop this mechanism (often called, rather vaguely, "voice building").

4—Study of music written for the voice, or of repertoire; this study is, of course, based upon one's ability to learn music and to perform it.

The secondary subjects may include:

1—Study of a keyboard instrument.
2—Study of stage deportment and acting.
3—Study of dancing, fencing, eurythmics, etc.
4—Study of the history of music and literature and of the various styles of music, literature and other arts.

Several of these subjects overlap. All of them complement one another. All of them are very important. A talented person, well trained in all of these subjects, would attain the synthesis of these various branches of his art and thus become not only an excellent singer, but an exceptionally efficient and cultured one besides.

Most people, however, are not usually fortunate enough to be able to receive such comprehensive training at a time when they could profit from it most. Many, if not most, for instance, have no idea that they wish to become singers and that they are sufficiently endowed to do so until they reach a comparative maturity. A comprehensive training in all the subjects outlined above is not easily completed in later years, since it may demand a very considerable period of time.

We know, however, that many talented people have managed to become excellent singers with rather scant training. Since this is so, it may be worth our while to examine how little of each subject a well-endowed singer needs to know to be able to perform. I feel obliged to repeat again, at the risk of becoming monotonously insistent, that a student who is poorly equipped by nature may expect to profit very little from all of these studies, no matter how serious, intense or comprehensive they may be. A student, however, with nothing but a good natural ear and a good natural voice, even though he may lack real talent, could improve considerably by pursuing such a curriculum.

Under ideal conditions, a singer ought to be expected to master thoroughly all the subjects outlined above. He ought to be a well-read and generally well-informed person besides. He ought to be well acquainted with other arts and have a general conception of disciplines of knowledge not pertaining to the arts and humanities, but ideal conditions are very rare indeed. Let us, therefore, set no maximum requirements for any branch of study necessary for singing, since every branch of such study is almost limitless. Let us try to discuss what the minimum requirements are.

When we consider the subjects of general musicianship in relation to singing, the first thing to remember is that a singer operates exclusively with only one line of music. In other words, pitch combinations hardly enter into his province for all practical purposes. His entire musical task is horizontal, not vertical like that of the pianist or organist.

No amount of theoretic studies can ever be considered as being "too much" in any branch of music, singing included. Ideally, therefore, every performing musician, including the singer, ought to know enough about music to be equipped to write a large symphonic work, whether he has any special gift for composition or not. Practically, however, a singer ought to concentrate on ear training, on sight singing and on primarily melodic dictation with especial emphasis on rhythm drills. Even the knowledge of harmony could, not that it should, be reduced to the aural familiarity with frequently encountered chords, with rules governing part-leading given only scant attention. Intense study of scales, intervals and rhythms could form a very efficient mainstay of the singer's musical

23

training. This study is anything but secondary for a singer although it is listed as such in many a music school catalogue. It ought to be pursued as intensively as it is humanly possible to do. Courses in sight singing and dictation especially designed for singers ought to be offered by every music school where singing is taught. Often such courses are not so designed; then problems of range, of primarily vertical dictation, and of insufficient drilling in rhythms make them very much less valuable to singers than they could be. Also, not enough time is devoted to them.

Training the ear of a singer should, in my opinion, begin with the most direct and least intellectualized procedure, namely by having the student sing, whistle or hum the pitches or series of pitches played for him on some musical instrument. Such training should precede any attempt at the reading of music. Naturally, such a type of training is not needed if the student shows an excellent ability to coordinate his ear, eye and voice. In most instances, however, the adoption of some such procedure would prove of considerable benefit to the student.

Most singers with a good natural ear seldom learn to read music efficiently, even many of those who graduate from accredited music schools. One reason for this is that they simply lack the time and opportunity to do so. An average singer often enters a music school with little knowledge of musical notation, and practically always with a very haphazard knowledge of it. He may have an excellent ear and a good natural voice. Now, in four or five years, he has to learn so much about music (including harmony, counterpoint, fugue, form, orchestration, piano, music history) that the simple, most elementary matters of basic ear training and basic familiarity with musical notation are lost in the shuffle. Obediently, he learns to put black dots on paper according to

rules, not even caring to imagine how they may sound. Obediently, he learns to control his fingers so that they can push
down keys in a properly pianistic manner though what this
has to do with his musical needs at this stage of his development no one seems to know. He memorizes dates and learns
musical nomenclature. He goes to a sight-singing class once
or twice a week, and, if he is called upon, sings assigned exercises with which he is already familiar and which often are
either too high or too low for his type of voice. He goes to
a dictation class and soon is confronted with complex vertical
music before he even had a chance to become thoroughly
familiarized with the notation of horizontal music. Besides all
this, he must learn three languages, go to dancing and acting
classes, take a few academic subjects if he wants a degree,
sing in a chorus and take voice lessons. It is obvious that such a
curriculum presupposes an exceptional ability plus very extensive preparatory work. Since vocal students usually lack the
latter requirement, the whole approach to this subject seems
to be in need of re-examination.

It seems to me that anyone who is sufficiently endowed
to consider the serious study of singing should first concentrate on training his ear, and, only after this task has been
successfully accomplished, should he begin to think in terms
of how to sing. A prospective singer who has a good musical
ear could attain a good command of musical notation necessary for his purposes in one year of concentrated study under
proper guidance. If he pursued such studies for several years,
he could easily reach a proficiency bordering on virtuosity.

It is true that many a fine singer has learned to sing without ever having mastered even the elements of musical notation. The mastery of musical notation is as important to a performing musician as a mastery of the elements of reading and
writing is important to anyone else. One *could* do without it,

it is true. Many a fine man has been illiterate and still managed to live a full and useful life. Literacy, as such, is not guaranteed to do anything for anyone except to make him literate. One can imagine an actor, superbly gifted and with the possession of an exceptional memory, of being illiterate. One can imagine a singer, equally superbly gifted and possessing an exceptional musical memory, of being musically illiterate. The advantage of being illiterate, however, escapes me in both instances.

The partisans of the view that unless a singer knows how to write a double fugue he cannot possibly call himself a musician, and the partisans of the view that a singer only needs to know how to produce melliferous sounds are equally unrealistic and shortsighted. I am most willing to admit that an exceptionally gifted singer may manage to perform without even knowing whether he should read the music from right to left or from left to right. However, I don't see how this admission would invalidate the contention that a singer needs to know as much about music as he can manage to learn. I do believe, however, that before he learns to write fugues, he must be sufficiently familiar with musical notation to be able to read at sight, faultlessly, a Schubert song. The fallacy of the advocates of "fugue writing" lies in the fact that they forget that anyone possessing a normal intelligence can manage to write a correct atrocity in fugue style without ever being able to distinguish a fourth from a fifth by ear. This fallacy results in an emphasis on paper work where musical theory is concerned. It results in granting degrees in music to singers who are not even equipped to distinguish one interval from another, simply because these people have managed to arrange black and white circles on ruled paper in a properly prescribed manner.

It is a singular and rather distressing fact that among

singers more than among any other performing musicians, one finds the two almost perverse extremes of musical illiteracy. One speaks of Debussy, Hugo Wolf and Bach, but he is not in the least disturbed by the fact that he may not be able even to sing a correct interval when asked to, much less read a piece of music accurately. The other bellows operatic airs, has to engage a coach to learn a line of music and is proud of his abysmal ignorance. The musically illiterate snob and the musically illiterate vulgarian who is proud of his illiteracy are both the products of the "fugue writing" mentality which still seems to be prevalent in most music schools. The snob "writes the fugue" and, consequently, considers himself a musician. The other sees that those who "write fugues" sing no better and sometimes worse than himself, remembers the tales of great singers who managed to sing beautifully despite the fact that they had no formal musical training, and consequently regards the entire subject of musical literacy as a superfluous affectation. That such utterly ridiculous specimens of ignorance can be found more readily among singers than among instrumentalists, seems to indicate that the manner in which general musicianship is being taught to singers is in great need of re-evaluation.

Unless we agree that the only possible approach to the teaching of music to a singer is by the way of his ear, we shall, I am afraid, continue to produce annually every conceivable variety of musical illiterates.

Were the knowledge of this obvious and, I am afraid, rather platitudinous point of view more widespread, children showing interest in singing would be encouraged to study ear training. Those failing to show signs of a good natural ear could then be steered toward the study of singing for their own personal enjoyment; for, unfortunately, although people with a poor natural ear can be found in all branches of music,

27

they seem to be most frequently encountered among singers. I must again repeat, *ad nauseam*, that the possession of a good natural ear does not, in itself, constitute the possession of a talent for music or for singing.

My position in regard to this matter could be summed up as follows: if a student of singing has a good musical ear, he should at first spend all of the time allotted to theoretic and allied subjects on ear training. Only when he has reached a comparative mastery of this subject may he proceed profitably with any theoretic studies which do not have a direct bearing upon his ability to imagine, recognize and reproduce pitches and rhythms. If, however, a singer has no musical ear, but he has learned either how to write fugues and canons or how to "place" his voice instead, he ought to be advised to pursue his studies on a purely amateur basis.

Since practically all of the available evidence seems to point in the direction that one's capacity to imagine pitches is inextricably connected with one's ability to produce them, I would advocate the study of ear training as the very first step in the study of singing. This study should precede, by at least a year, any attempt at vocalization. It should be considered a major study and treated as such by both the student and the teacher. Failure to attain marked proficiency in it after a specified period of time should definitely signify a natural inaptitude for singing.

III. The Study of the Verbal Contents in Vocal Music

When we consider the next major subject dealing with another facet of singing, namely with the verbal contents of vocal music, we cannot deal with it as summarily as we did with the facet of singing dealing with the study of pitches and rhythms. We cannot reduce this subject to a workable minimum as easily and as honestly unless we radically change the conception of singing which, for better or for worse, is prevalent in English-speaking countries.

When a singer is supposed to perform in four languages, as English-speaking singers are expected to do, a mastery of those four languages seems to be clearly indicated. The demand that a singer perform equally well in four languages could be likened in its reasonableness to a demand that every actor perform equally well in English, French, German and Italian. Each language has its phonetic peculiarities. Each language has its own rhythm and inflection. Each language demands a different variety of muscular coordinations necessary for the production of its own particular speech sounds, and each language demands its own system of "ear training" if such coordination is to be attained. Considered in this light, the attainment of the most minimal linguistic requirements necessary for singing would entail a great deal of study. That few enough English-speaking singers ever attain a mastery of

French, German and Italian equal to the mastery of their own native language, is an eloquent testimony to the difficulty under which the English-speaking singer is made to labor by the convention prevalent today.

A French singer learns to sing in French, and, unless he is very ambitious and especially interested in singing in German, Italian or English, he keeps on singing in French for the rest of his career. Of course, he may learn some songs or arias in Italian or German if he wishes to or if he believes such a procedure would be helpful. If he decides not to do so, he still may sing only in his native language and not be considered an artistic pariah because of this. The same attitude is prevalent in Germany, Italy, Russia and practically every other country in continental Europe. However, it is unfortunately not accepted as desirable in Great Britain, the United States or other English-speaking countries. The reasons for this nonacceptance are not difficult to establish historically.

Aesthetically, the practice can be defended with some vigor on the one hand but assailed with perhaps even greater vigor on the other. Every advocate of singing in the original language must grant that good vocal music consists of music and words of which neither takes undue precedence over the other. He must agree that the meaning of the words and not only their sound greatly influences the music, and thus plays an integral part in the enjoyment of it. How then is one to defend singing in French, German and Italian to an audience composed of people who do not understand any of these languages by a singer who usually knows hardly more about them save some fundamental rules of their pronunciation?

It is true that if one knows French, for instance, or Finnish, one would prefer hearing a French or a Finnish song in its original form, but I, for one, not knowing a word of Finnish, seem to enjoy less listening to Finnish songs in their original language than if they were sung in a language I happen to understand. The crowning and somewhat ludicrous exhibition of the confusion which seems to affect the linguistic matters of singing in English-speaking countries is the rather frequent spectacle of an English-speaking artist singing a Russian song, not in an English but in a French translation and for the benefit of an audience that doesn't know a word of French.

A linguistically gifted person may gain, within two years, a workable knowledge of a new language, particularly if he is living in the country where this language is spoken. He must be an exceptionally linguistically gifted individual to do nearly as well if he stays at home. Learning a language is, after all, primarily a matter of ear. Some people with no musical ear whatsoever have an excellent ear for speech sounds. Some again possess a good musical ear and have little capacity for imagining new speech sounds.

It is not necessary to concern oneself with niceties of style of grammar in order to learn a language in a workable manner. A fundamental grammatical survey will do very well. The rest is picked up by ear. An English-speaking singer, therefore, if he is to take the convention of singing in four languages seriously, ought to spend some six years in continental Europe. This, of course, is a matter of finances and of time. If one can afford it, it is a splendid idea, but most students simply cannot expect to pursue such an expensive way of studying. The overwhelming majority must stay at home and try to learn the languages in a classroom.

Let us examine the manner in which languages seem to be taught in most of the music schools. Language, as an academic subject, is the medium by which one increases his ability to come in contact with the culture of a foreign country. The aim of such an approach to linguistic study necessitates an emphasis on grammar and vocabulary. A student who success-fully accomplishes such a study must be able to read and understand a book, a newspaper or a poem in a foreign language without having to thumb through a dictionary at every line. Still and all, the practical aim of a singer's study of a language is not to gain its comprehensive use, although it is an ideal aim, but rather to learn to produce the proper speech sounds and to learn to translate a song text with any and every help that he may summon. Again, I must admit that it would be preferable if an English-speaking singer who sings in French, Italian and German could read and write freely in these languages. A music school is not precisely the place where he might look for such training. Languages in most of the music schools are secondary subjects, and perhaps rightly so. Not much time is allotted to these studies, and yet the overwhelming majority of such language classes is conducted as if the acquisition of a comprehensive knowledge of a language is intended. Grammar and vocabulary drills take up most of the time. The net result is negligible because of the insufficient time allotted and because of the rather natural impatience on the part of the vocal student with matters such as irregular verbs. The knowledge of grammar gained by an average vocal student in such a class would not enable him to understand a headline in a foreign-language newspaper. The knowledge of vocabulary is even more inadequate for his needs, since the vocabulary used in operatic librettos or song texts has little to do with ordering one's breakfast or engaging a room in a hotel. This utterly unrealistic approach to a singer's linguistic training poorly prepares most English-speaking vocal students for the task ahead of them.

An intensive study of pronunciation should occupy most of the time allotted to language classes in music schools. The vocabulary used for such study should be drawn directly from the standard opera and song texts of each language. It does not matter how old-fashioned, obsolete or florid it may seem compared to the modern vocabulary. Grammar ought to be taken as nonchalantly as possible. If a singer can translate a song text, word for word, with all the help a dictionary and a table of irregular verbs and declensions can offer him, he will know enough grammar for his immediate purposes. An enormous stress should be laid on reciting the opera and song texts in class.

Many "diction" classes ("pronunciation" is the correct word, but "diction" is very frequently used instead) in German, French and Italian adopt a procedure whereby a student is required to sing in class and is then corrected for pronunciation. This is a very unrealistic manner in which to attack the problem. Until a student learns the speech sound as such, he cannot easily combine it with pitch, rhythm and vocalized tone. As very advanced work in pronunciation this procedure would work excellently. As an introductory or intermediate study of pronunciation, it tends to create an undue amount of tension in the student. This tension is due to the fact that he is expected, at one and the same time, to pronounce a word with which he is not quite familiar, to sing it on a pitch and in a rhythm pattern he may not be too sure of and to sing it in a manner demanded by his vocal teacher, a manner he is just managing to acquire. This approach to "diction" usually results in some musical and often considerable psychological and vocal damage to the student. To be able to sing a pitch one must first be able to hear it inside one's head. The same rule applies to words. The new speech sounds should first be introduced by the teacher as sounds and not as mechanical exercises in tongue and lip movement, and then they should be tried by each student for exactly as long as it is necessary for him to imitate the teacher. Insufficient elementary aural

33

drilling in the sounds of a language, and the unnecessary and confusing drilling in tongue and lip movements, verb forms and endings, make most of the language classes in music schools ineffective in so far as vocal students are concerned. If, again, the entire subject were re-examined on a more realistic and utilitarian basis, the results of such classes would be more in harmony with their aims.

It is my contention, however, that the study of general phonetics, of standard English pronunciation and of recitation of poetry and prose passages in English should precede the study of any foreign language. Again, I base my contention on the similarity of process involved in producing pitch and word. To begin with, a singer must learn to synchronize speech sounds with pitches. How can he manage this much if he cannot summon a clear image of the speech sound in his mind because this speech sound is unfamiliar to his ear? If he does manage to do so, he must do so in a tense, mechanical manner which will affect both the sound of the word and the quality of the pitch. But synchronization of word and pitch is not all that is demanded of a singer. The pitch, besides being accurate, must form a part of a rhythmic pattern and must be produced in an agreeable manner vocally. The word, besides being correctly pronounced, must have an inflection (or "tone of voice"), since it forms a part of a sentence. The verbal sentence must be synchronized with a musical sentence. The musical sentence in the vocal line must be synchronized with the musical sentence of the accompanying instrument.

How can an individual who is unsure of the entire process even attempt this complex synchronization, if the speech sounds, their meaning and their inflection are in a language totally unfamiliar to him or nearly so? I would venture to suggest that if this process of synchronization were being learned in a familiar language, the problem would definitely be simplified and the necessary synchronization acquired much more easily. A singer who cannot recite a song text with proper conversational inflection (that is, in a manner where the logic of the sentence is clearly presented to the listener, where punctuation is observed, where words of greater importance receive greater emphasis) cannot hope to learn to phrase a song. Phrasing of most vocal music is based upon the meaning of a sentence, and its effect upon the inflection with which one recites this sentence and sings the corresponding musical part. A singer who must think of how to pull or push his lips into proper position to produce a certain vowel or consonant, instead of knowing it by ear, cannot hope to acquire any ease in his production of this sound and cannot therefore expect to sing it in any normal tone of voice. It seems, therefore, obvious that unless a singer knows the speech sounds of a foreign language thoroughly by ear, this language ought not to be used for vocalizing purposes.

English is as good a language to sing in as any other, provided it is the singer's native language. It may seem a very unsingable language to an Italian, but then Italian may seem equally unsingable to an American student who cannot produce a clear Italian "u" sound, since never in his life has he used one. Why could not an English-speaking student learn to sing (that is, to synchronize the musical and verbal contents of a song in a vocally agreeable manner) in his own language, and only after such synchronization has taken root, proceed with other languages? He may study the other languages most intensively at the same time without trying to sing in them.

This suggestion differs radically from a rather prevalent idea that one should learn to sing in Italian first whether one is familiar with the language or not. The practice of learning to sing in Italian in preference to one's own language has deep

35

roots in the history of singing in England. I do not see, however, why a practice which may have had some reason in eighteenth-century England should still be adhered to today. Such a practice prevailed in seventeenth-century Germany, but it has long since been discarded and with no apparent ill effects.

The acquisition of a standardized manner in which one uses his lips and tongue in his own language is of fundamental importance to any prospective singer, and will have a most definite bearing on the ease with which he may learn to pronounce and sing foreign words. The fundamentals of speech should definitely be considered as one of the primary subjects in a vocal student's curriculum, and it should be pursued most intensively during the first year of his studies or until it is fully mastered.

Likewise, the acquisition of control over inflection in speech should occupy every prospective singer most seriously, since inflection or the tone of voice is, perhaps, his most important tool of expression. An instrumentalist, though able to produce a much greater number of pitches than any singer and to produce them more rapidly and more accurately, can operate only with volume, rhythm and limited varieties of tone color for expressive purposes. A human voice is capable of an infinite variety of inflections. It is, unfortunately, only too true that but few singers are able to use any variety of inflection while singing. This fact may be directly attributed to the almost complete lack of interest, and therefore of practice, in training oneself to coordinate speech inflection with singing. Only singers of popular songs seem invariably to excel in this accomplishment, since they cannot hide a monotonous delivery of the text behind a respectable façade of *bel canto*. Recitation of a song text should, therefore, seem to be a most needed preparation to the singing of a song. That it is seldom practiced by singers and, to my knowledge, not often demanded from them by most teachers or schools, is a singularly unfortunate oversight which is often responsible for the extraordinarily stilted, unnatural and senseless manner in which so many poems are handled when they are being sung.

The polylingual approach to singing often produces many other peculiar consequences among English-speaking vocal students. Many of them, for instance, are so concerned with the problems which the pronunciation of foreign languages present, that they fail to pay enough attention to clarity of enunciation when they sing in their native tongue. The fact that they understand and know the sound of each word when they sing in English seems to absolve them from any responsibility for a clear and precise delivery of an English text. It is also not uncommon to hear English-speaking students transfer some of the phonetic characteristics of Italian and German into their own language so that, after a while, they begin to sing in English with a rather pronounced foreign accent.

I should like to sum up my suggestions. A student of singing could proceed with his speech studies in a very efficient manner if:

1—He learns first the fundamental principles of speech and phonetics as applied to his own language.

2—He learns to recite the texts intelligently in his own language before attempting to sing them.

3—He learns to use his singing voice efficiently in his own language first.

4—He becomes thoroughly familiar with the speech sounds of a foreign language before, not while, he attempts to sing in it.

5—He becomes thoroughly familiar with the meaning of a text of a foreign song and learns to recite it properly before, not while, he attempts to learn to sing it.

IV. The Study of Vocal Technic

Any discussion of vocal technic (voice placement or tone production as it is often called) is doomed, at some point or other, to become controversial. A spirit of partisanship seems to be evoked by such discussions most of the time. Apparently it cannot be banished by any known method of dealing with the subject.

It is not my aim to instruct the reader in vocal technic. A staggering number of volumes written for just such purpose already exists. I do not see the need for adding still another to this list. The purpose of this chapter then is to discuss some fundamental premises upon which an approach to the study of vocal technic could rest.

The aim of vocal technic, as of all musical performance technics, is to enable the singer to produce at will and with reasonable ease, sounds of specified pitch, duration, quality, volume, color, etc. Any intelligent approach toward the achievement of this aim must rest on a clear understanding of the nature and limitation of the instrument as well as on a clear understanding of the nature and limitations of the procedures available for teaching the attainment of control of this instrument.

It is my sincere belief that, should these two major premises be sufficiently explored, the student would gain

38

enough insight into the subject to become able to form an approach to the study of vocal technic which would fit his individual needs.

As discussed before, the factor primarily responsible for the production of any specified sound by a normal human voice is the conception of a clear mental image of this sound. The formation of this mental image compels our sound-producing mechanism to adjust itself in a most minute and delicate manner; it sets in motion a most complex series of muscular contractions balanced to a most remarkable degree of precision which results in an approximation of the imagined sound. The control of this factor (the conception of sound image) rests primarily upon the degree of precision with which an individual can imagine sounds at will. The natural ability to imagine sounds of definite pitch at will has already been discussed. In its lowest form, this ability enables one to imagine sounds of definite duration, pitch, vowel and volume. In its highest form, this ability enables one to imagine sound in its full complexity. Quality, intensity, timbre, resonance, inflection and every other characteristic of musical sound produced in conjunction with speech sound by a human voice must be imagined before any worthwhile attempt can be made to produce it successfully.

Insofar as speech is concerned, the formation of a sound image and its reproduction in an adult reaches a state of such automatism that the meaning of a word becomes synonymous with its sound. Thus the sound becomes an automatic expression of the meaning. The same automatism, if attained by a singer, will form his most valuable attribute as an artist. To attain such automatism, in which the meaning of the word, the sound of the word and the musical sound form a simultaneous and instantaneous single image, is the higher goal of a singer's technic.

39

The ability to imagine sound is of equally paramount importance where every conceivable sound which can be produced by a human voice is concerned. The possession of this ability, insofar as speech is concerned, makes it possible for the same actor to change the color, inflection, quality and volume of his voice. It enables him to change the accent and rhythm of his speech so that one night his words will sound as he imagines the speech of Romeo should sound, and the next night approximate his image of the speech of a New York taxi driver. It makes it possible for those possessing a very keen ear for speech sounds to imitate the speech peculiarities, inflections and accents of innumerable individuals. Also, it makes it possible for those who have a very keen ear for sounds produced by animals and birds somehow to approximate these sounds. Finally, it makes it possible for those who have a very keen ear for musical sounds to reproduce the sounds they imagine in conjunction with speech sounds, or to sing.

The possession of such an ability is not, however, synonymous with the possession of a voice which would allow the approximation of any imagined sound. A limited or inferior voice, as well as one of superior or extraordinary nature, is the result of a most complex combination of physical and mental factors which, for all practical purposes, could be considered accidental. The limitations of each individual's voice cannot be discounted. Imagining a sound out of the range of one's voice or beyond its maximum volume will not, of course, result in the approximation of this sound. Imagining a sound of a quality which the individual voice is incapable of reproducing due to its structure, cannot be expected to result in an approximation of this quality.

It seems to me that no approach to the study of vocal technic can ignore the principle that the major portion of the control a singer possesses over his voice rests on his ability to imagine in its full complexity the sound which he wishes to produce—that is, in its pitch, vowel, duration, quality, volume, resonance, timbre, inflection, color, etc. If the characteristics of a sound the singer wishes to produce are unclear in his own mind, little if anything can be done to compel him to produce successfully a sound possessing such characteristics. This remains true even if his vocal apparatus should be of a structure which theoretically could allow him to produce such a sound at will; for the muscles primarily responsible for the production of a sound—namely, the vocal cords—are, for all practical purposes, uncontrollable as such insofar as direct volition is concerned. Although not classified as involuntary muscles (like the heart or the intestines,) neither are they classified as voluntary muscles (such as the biceps).

We do not possess the faculty of compelling our vocal cords to flex in any precise manner without first having conceived an image of the sound we wish to produce. This is a fact of cardinal importance, a fact which has an enormous bearing upon any approach toward the study of vocal technic.

Certain parts of our complex sound-producing apparatus can be controlled, as such, to a greater or lesser degree. These include the tongue, the lips and the muscles of the jaw as well as a great number of other sets of muscles distributed in various parts of the body and involved to some degree in the production of a sound. However, the primary sound-producing muscles, the vocal cords, which are responsible for the pitch of a sound and for much of its quality, can be *only* controlled by indirect action. This indirect action depends entirely upon the singer's ability to imagine or hear mentally, the sound that he wishes to produce.

The functioning of most other muscles that form or are indirectly related to our sound-producing apparatus is often semiautomatic and invariably is influenced by the image of sound we conceive mentally. It is also affected by the concurrent activity of all the other sets of muscles employed in producing a sound. None of such muscles or sets of muscles operates independently of each other while a sound is being produced, for neither of them alone is capable of emitting a vowel sound of a definite pitch, quality, volume or color.

It seems obvious, therefore, that the most precise knowledge of the muscular contractions involved in the production of some specified sound cannot be expected to make a singer produce this sound accurately, since the accurate mental image of the desired sound is the factor primarily responsible for compelling these muscles to act. The most minutely accurate knowledge of all the muscular activities involved in the production of a middle C on vowel "a," for instance, cannot enable one to compel directly his muscles to contract in so precise a manner as to insure even an approximation of this specified sound unless one conceives a mental image of this sound or, at the very least, of its pitch and vowel.

The student of singing should bear in mind that his sound producing mechanism invariably acts as a complex unit. He must remember that the exact balancing of the multitude of muscular activities responsible for the emission of any specified sound cannot be successfully achieved by direct muscular effort. The conception of an image of the sound can, however, successfully coordinate, unify and direct these complex muscular contractions.

Much too often, one encounters a total disregard of this principle among students trying to attain control over their vocal apparatus. Too many of them seem to reason in some such fashion as this: No specified sound can be produced unless a series of certain muscular contractions takes place. The approach to the study of vocal technic should, in accordance with this premise, rest primarily on analyzing these muscular contractions. Armed with such knowledge, one is supposed to be able to reproduce these muscular contractions at will. The reproduction of these muscular contractions will, according to this reasoning, result in the approximation of a desired sound. Accordingly, such series of muscular contractions are considered to be the sole cause of the desired sound.

Such reasoning confuses the cause with the effect. This type of mistake in reasoning is very frequently encountered. Effect (in this case muscular activity) is often mistaken for the cause (in this case conception of the sound image) and the attempt to gain control over the effect is then considered to be equal to the attempt to gain control over the cause. Singing in this manner, a student can lose most of his natural coordination. He will become self-conscious; he will forget what it means to allow himself to make music naturally; and the more talented he is, the more chance there will be for him to develop innumerable mental blocks which may, in the end, prevent him from singing altogether.

A student with a poor natural ear, a poor natural voice and no imagination can, of course, be taught how to force himself into squeaking a semblance of a high C, for instance (which he may not have been able to do before) if he is shown precisely how to open his mouth, in what manner to hold his tongue, in what fashion to flex his abdominal muscles and so on. The result, of course, will be utterly unsatisfactory insofar as singing goes, but it may enable him to produce a semblance of a high C. A student of some talent, however, if taught to employ the same mechanical devices while singing a high C, stands to gain nothing by forcing himself to act as an untalented singer does, and may, in the process of learning how to sing in this fashion, do permanent damage to his whole way of singing and his attitude toward the act of singing. In the end, he may, and often does, learn to sing no better than the ungifted student.

Under such training he learns how *not* to develop his gift (whatever this gift may be) and not to rely upon any natural aptitude he may have for singing. Before long, unless he happens to be a most exceptionally gifted and strong individual, he may, because of disuse and abuse of his natural basic coordination, lose it altogether.

The old complaint of parents and friends that "Jenny or Peggy or Tommy used to sound much better until he or she went to New York or Chicago or Los Angeles and began to study singing" is, unfortunately, all too often justified, but, just as unfortunately, nothing much is ever done about it. Jenny or Peggy or Tommy simply insist that the "old way" of singing was "all wrong" but that the new way, even though it makes them sound like sputtering steam whistles, is "correct," and that they simply did not quite get the hang of it as yet, and need to study more "vocal technic," meaning, of course, more mechanical devices designed to teach one how to control consciously and directly the muscles of one's sound-producing apparatus.

A student who becomes convinced that vocal technic is purely a matter of direct gymnastic muscular control, and that such vocal technic equals singing, is often willing to admit that his present way of singing may be unsatisfactory. But it seems very difficult for such a student to realize that his vocal inefficiency is primarily due to his general conception of what vocal technic is, and to his general attitude toward the act of singing. It seems difficult for him to perceive that exchanging one system of direct muscular control for another such system (which he is often willing to do) will not essentially alleviate his plight. It may possibly increase

44

it. It is extremely difficult for him to understand that his inefficiency is due not to the type of gymnastic muscular control he tries to employ in his singing, but to the fact that such direct gymnastic muscular control is being employed at all.

Many a gifted student in search of some hypothetical type of direct muscular control which he calls "vocal technic," and which he hopes will finally release him and allow him to sing freely and efficiently, goes from one voice specialist to another and changes his vocal technic with each new teacher. Such a student does not seem to consider the possibility that no type of direct muscular control can make him sing as he wishes to sing, and as perhaps he could sing, unless the mental and musical factors governing the operation of his muscles are allowed to play the extraordinarily important part in his singing, a part to which such factors are rightfully entitled.

I do not wish to imply that a student of singing cannot and should not learn how to gain direct control over certain voluntary muscles involved in singing if such control seems necessary. However, the often-encountered overemphasis on direct muscular control among vocal students is almost invariably responsible for the increase of tension in their singing. This acquired tension sometimes reaches a stage where the singer becomes muscle-bound and is unable to sing as well and as easily as he did before he began to study seriously, and to concern himself with the position of the larynx or the back of his tongue, his uvula or his diaphragm. It is not surprising then that those studentts who become most muscle-bound are those most concerned with their muscular activities and least conscious of the function of the mental sound image, which, under normal circumstances, would tend to

45

direct and coordinate their muscular activities. They must, of necessity, neglect to concentrate on the sound image while their attention is riveted to the minute muscular details of their singing.

I would venture to say that the acquisition of direct control even over voluntary muscles may be resorted to only when the natural coordination between the student's ear and his voice seems insufficient to insure the approximation of the desired sound. This, of course, presupposes that the student knows or has been taught to know what precisely a desired sound may be and that he can actually imagine this sound clearly. Before this has been tried and found wanting, the preoccupation with direct muscular control can only result in disturbing whatever natural coordination the student has between his ear and his voice.

To sum up: The primary control a singer possesses over his instrument is not muscular but mental. It rests on a natural ability to imagine musical and speech sounds precisely, as well as on the natural coordination between the singer's ear and his voice. This ability, this supplementary coordination, and a vocal apparatus of a structure which enables the singer to reproduce the sounds he imagines are characteristics which cannot be acquired by study for any practical professional purposes. If such characteristics are present, however, they can be developed. Any intelligent approach toward the acquisition of an efficient vocal technic must take this into account. The acquisition of direct conscious control over certain muscles involved in producing sounds can be considered only as a supplementary, secondary aim in the study of vocal technic. It is often considered as the primary aim of vocal technic and substituted for the mental control of one's vocal apparatus by means of forming a sound image. An attempt to acquire such muscular control in a gymnastic, mechanical fashion usually disturbs the natural coordination between a student's voice and his ear. In other words, it makes his singing less efficient.

An insufficient realization of the extraordinarily important part which the formation of a thoroughly accurate mental sound image plays in one's singing is often responsible for a number of the so-called "technical difficulties" among students of singing. Many, if not most, of such vocal ills plaguing a young singer are very often due to the inefficient musical, verbal and phonetic preparation of the pieces he attempts to sing. In other words, only few of them mentally know well enough the music, the poem and the vowel and consonant sounds of the song they attempt to sing before they actually begin to sing it. Unless a student is taught to be extremely precise in learning to imagine the sound of the musical and phonetic content of his songs before he begins to sing them, he usually forms the very poor habit of learning his songs by singing them before he knows them well enough to hear them mentally. Such a procedure is likely to impede the coordination between his ear and his voice or, to make him employ this coordination in a most minimal, haphazard and inefficient manner.

This insecurity in pitch, rhythm and phonetics is often responsible for a total inefficiency in vocalization among young singers. Also, this insecurity is often primarily responsible for the extraordinary tension of their vocal apparatus. A student who attempts to compel his vocal apparatus to produce pitches, rhythms and speech sounds of which he is not too sure must remember that his vocal apparatus will invariably become extremely tense in protest against such abuse. This tense, constricted sensation is only aggravated if the cause of this insecurity is not removed. Even the most specific advice on how to relax certain muscles and flex others while singing cannot then perceptibly lessen such tension.

Learning the notes and the words of a song is equivalent to making oneself hear them mentally. Attempting to do so while singing almost invariably tends to establish a peculiarly unnatural coordinatory pattern in one's singing. One's inner ear (or the ability to imagine sounds) is used hardly at all and never for any considerable length of time. One's vocal apparatus is thus left without proper mental guidance. This is especially noticeable in difficult passages where utmost concentration on pitch, vowel, quality, intensity and volume of a series of sounds is demanded in order to provide the needed guidance to the voice and ease the physical tension. It matters little if the student has, by that time, learned the tune and the words, or has even managed somehow to memorize them in this unnatural fashion. Doing so he has also managed to memorize a whole series of tense and uncomfortable sensations caused by the initially insecure knowledge of his piece. The music, the words and these tense and uncomfortable sensations become in this fashion welded into a unified pattern which he now calls singing.

Under such circumstances, the student begins to accept the sensation of tenseness as a sort of natural ill. Many believe that this tension cannot be corrected without years of study of the vocal mechanics and of gymnastic exercises especially designed to counteract it. Yet they seem to forget that the more conscious the student becomes of this tenseness and of the various corrective exercises, "trick" and "technics" designed to correct it, the less attention he begins to pay to the musical and verbal components of his work. His attention is then riveted to his body and not to the combined image of music and words before him. In this way he adds self-consciousness to the tension initially caused by the failure to form a sufficiently clear and secure mental image of what he is supposed to sing. This self-consciousness, in its turn, makes him even more tense. More mechanical devices designed to correct this self-consciousness are then employed with equally poor results until the student, as it so often unfortunately happens, cannot any longer produce a sound without enormous physical difficulty.

At this point I would like briefly to discuss practicing, as it is conceived by many vocal students. Most vocal students seem to believe that unless they sing they do not practice. Nothing could be more unrealistic. The primary purpose of practicing is to acquaint one's inner ear with the sound or the series of sounds one wishes to produce; the secondary purpose is to try to approximate this already imagined sound or series of sounds with one's voice, and to experiment with this process. It seems to me that a vocal student ought not to allow himself to sing until, to the best of his ability, he has arrived at some definite image of the sound or the series of sounds he wishes to produce. Singing before having formed such an image will only confuse the student. It can be safely said that perhaps more harm is done to the average student by his *own* senseless and haphazard way of practicing than by anything else.

Most students, even those who are exceptionally efficient in learning music by looking at it and who know the languages in which they sing well enough to be able to speak, read and write in them, would do much toward the elimination of this possible cause of many of their vocal ills by adopting the following procedure in learning a song:

> *1*—Learn the poem separately. Translate it word for word if it is in a language with which you are not overly familiar. Check every syllable of it for correct pronuncia-

tion, and for accurate vowel sounds over and over until you are able to imagine precisely every speech sound involved. Practice speaking it aloud until it seems phonetically perfect, and until you can speak it without any strain. Then learn to recite it as a piece of poetry so that the sense of it may be immediately grasped by anyone familiar with the language. Search for the right inflection in each sentence. Do not begin learning the music until you have mastered the verbal content of the song to your best ability.

2—Learn the rhythmic pattern of the vocal line separately from the pitch pattern by tapping it out or by using some syllable such as "la" to indicate it. This, of course, is not absolutely necessary for those who have developed a precise and reliable manner of translating signs indicating rhythms into audible rhythmic patterns. Many singers, however, would profit by such separate examination of the rhythmic contents of their music.

3—Synchronize the poem and the rhythmic pattern to which it has been set by the composer by learning to recite the poem in strict and precise time.

4—Learn the pitches of the vocal line. Again, those who are able to hear music by looking at it will not need to spend much time on such an elementary task. Few singers have been sufficiently trained in sight singing, however, to be justified in taking this task too lightly. The only way to learn the pitches and rhythms of a vocal line is to learn to hear them. If one's eye and ear coordination is inefficient, as it usually is in a singer with average training, it should not be strained by an impractical attempt to learn to sight sing on the song one wishes eventually to perform. It would be much more realistic to learn to hear the vocal line of such a song by playing it in strict time on the piano with one finger, and by repeating this process until one can mentally hear each phrase with utmost exactitude.

Most singers do not play the piano well enough to play the accompaniment accurately. I should, therefore, discourage them from trying to do so, since it is better to learn to hear the vocal line precisely and in time instead of forming a confused image of it in a jumble of inaccurate chords played in slovenly rhythm. Naturally, if the student is able to acquaint himself with the chordal structure of the accompaniment by playing it in an accurate, simplified version of his own, it will help him immensely to learn to hear mentally the vocal line. But even though the most exhaustive knowledge of the accompaniment of a song is imperative to the singer, he should not attempt to gain such knowledge on his own unless he happens to be an efficient pianist.

One should not attempt to sing the vocal line in any fashion until one can hear it mentally precisely on pitch and in rhythm note for note.

5—Only after speech sounds, rhythms and pitches of a vocal line have been thoroughly absorbed by the student may he attempt to vocalize this melody on some vowel which he deems best for such purposes. The vocalization should be metronomically precise.

6—Sing the words of the song in strict time but on monotone. Choose any pitch which seems most comfortable for such a purpose.

7—Put the song away for a few hours. After this, you will be able to practice it without doing damage to it as well as to your voice.

51

Another serious misconception of the nature of the singer's instrument which produces very undesirable consequences is the idea that a singer must try to hear himself sing, or form an idea of what his singing sounds like to his listeners. We all know that we cannot form an adequate idea of how our speech sounds to others. Anyone who has ever had his speech recorded will know the shock he experiences on hearing such a recording for the first time. It is difficult to realize that the speech peculiarities which we hear on the record could actually be our own. Singing is a form of musicalized speech. The musical part of the singing is produced by the same instrument that produces the speech. I do not see how the inability to hear one's own speech as it sounds to others will be lessened by adding pitch and rhythm to the speech sounds. It seems to me that this unrealistic advice, which many singers unfortunately try to follow, stems from instrumental musicians. Instrumentalists can hear themselves as others hear them, and endeavor to do so to the utmost of their ability. A singer, however, who tries to follow the same procedure as an instrumentalist in this matter will create a number of grave difficulties for himself.

As soon as the singer tries to listen to the sound he is producing, the functioning of his inner ear (or his ability to imagine sounds) becomes less efficient, all of which is equivalent to saying that his vocal apparatus is left temporarily with little or no guidance. The sound can then continue to remain accurate only if the vocal apparatus is to a greater or lesser degree kept forcibly in the same position by direct muscular effort. This will immediately produce unnecessary muscular tension, and will affect adversely the quality of the sound, the inflection and the general manner of delivery. If such "clamping" of the voice is not resorted to, the pitch as well as the vowel may change markedly during the period in which the singer tries to concentrate on the evaluation of the sound he is producing instead of concentrating on the image of the sound he wishes to produce.

Such post-factum listening accomplishes no purpose. It distracts the singer's attention from his immediate task, thus affecting the accuracy of singing by disturbing the coordinatory pattern between his inner ear and his voice. It offers nothing in return.

An instrumentalist, however, can manage to continue producing a sound while listening to it and evaluating it. He can keep his fingers in some definite position without becoming overly tense. He can do so because the production of a sound on most musical instruments does not depend totally on the continuous presence of the sound image in his mind.

One must bear in mind that the possession of a good musical ear does not, in itself, insure accuracy and ease in singing. Without such an ear, a singer cannot hope to attain accuracy or freedom, but even when he possesses an excellent ear he must train himself to use it to advantage. Those who are preoccupied with trying to listen to and evaluate the sound they are producing, those who are unduly preoccupied with the mechanical means which they deem necessary for attaining some quality of sound which may appeal to them, those who are preoccupied with eliminating the symptoms of undesirable tension by some mechanical means which do not take into account the very cause of such tension, all of such singers deliberately abuse and misuse the functioning of their musical ear. It is not surprising, therefore, that some singers with an extraordinarily keen natural ear sing miserably off pitch, are aware of it afterward, and are unable to correct their intonation.

It is a common misconception among vocal students to attribute inaccuracy of pitch to some mechanical factor and thus to seek some mechanical means of correction. This misconception, as well as the one concerning listening to oneself instead of concentrating on the image of the sound one wishes to produce, stems from the instrumental conception of music making. A string player, for instance, can correct his intonation by shifting his finger ever so little. A singer can never gage the precise muscular action necessary for such a correction. He must hear the precise pitch inside his mind to be able to set in motion and coordinate the multitude of muscular activities necessary for such a minute adjustment.

Vocal students often make a distinction between singing "off pitch" and singing "off color" and often maintain that this "off color" singing is due to some mechanical causes and not to a lack of accuracy of the sound image they form mentally. This, of course, is nothing but quibbling. "Color," insofar as it can affect pitch, is an integral part of the pitch. If the singer is unable to imagine the proper color so as to produce the accurate pitch, the chances are that he is either not able mentally to hear it accurately enough or that he does not concentrate hard enough to hear it; for one can sing very "brightly" and be flat, and very "darkly" and be sharp, as all of us, no doubt, have found out from experience.

One must remember that the pitch of a sound has little to do with its quality or its beauty. On may produce very ugly sounds very accurately on pitch and very beautiful sounds very much off pitch. Speaking of sound color in terms of pitch seems to indicate an arbitrary differentiation in degrees of inaccuracy. In this fashion, off color serves to indicate a slight inaccuracy while off pitch is meant to describe a glaring deviation from the intended pitch.

The study of vocal technic differs enormously in some respects from the study of instrumental technic. To be able to play a scale in the worst possible manner on any instrument requires a modicum of conscious muscular control. This is due to the fact that the ability to hear inside oneself what is musically required does not produce even the lowest form of muscular coordination necessary for its execution on any musical instrument. However, anyone who can hear a scale clearly can manage to sing it after a fashion. Therefore, every normal person who can carry a tune possesses a vocal technic which could be termed as being equivalent to the instrumental technic acquired by an average instrumentalist in two or three years of study. This is often completely disregarded by both the student and the teacher. A vocal student needs all the musical and speech training he can get to enable him to catch up with his elementary vocal technic while an instrumentalist must learn muscular control and concentrate on it before he can catch up with his natural musical ability.

This disparity between a natural technic which a singer learns in speaking and can use for singing, and the lack of such a natural technic which every young instrumentalist must overcome, lessens by the time the singer and the instrumentalist go beyond the elementary stage of their development. However, the idea that a student of singing needs to be instructed in the elements of muscular mechanics to the same degree as does a student of an instrument seems rather far-fetched and illogical.

A premature concentration on vocal mechanics too often tends to make a singer self-conscious and afraid to rely on the natural coordination between his voice and his ear. When this happens, the entire basis on which vocal technic could be developed is destroyed even though the student may have superior ear, voice and talent.

In my opinion the cornerstones of any approach to the study of vocal technic should be: 1) The strengthening of this natural coordination; 2) The increase of reliance upon it in the singer; 3) Forming the habit of guiding his voice primarily by means of his own inner ear; and 4) Forming the habit of employing conscious muscular effort only in a subsidiary, complementary manner and then only if such effort does not impede his natural coordination.

When and if such an approach is not employed by the student, we see the spectacle of naturally well-endowed singers unable to make use of their gifts. The longer they study what they call "vocal technic" the more difficult it seems for them to sing. The more they know about the mechanics of their voices, the less successfully they can manage to do those things which they did before they had studied. As a rule it is not their fault or the fault of their teacher. It is simply a result of the attitude which refuses to recognize that a vocal student should first be made conscious of what to want to do before he can hope to find a way of doing it. He cannot be taught successfully how to execute precisely something which is not overly clear in his own mind. The very nature of his instrument does not allow him to do so. This attitude toward the pedagogics of singing has destroyed and stunted more talented singers than perhaps any other factor.

I should like to add here that learning how to form a series of accurate images of the sounds one wishes to produce may be an extremely tedious and difficult task, one demanding considerable practice and a great degree of self discipline. It requires at first the utmost of concentration—the kind of concentration which can sometimes be attained only by trying to make one's mind totally blank and by substituting a continuous series of sound images for all thought.

Most singers allow their minds to wander while they sing. After initially having mentally heard, for a fraction of a second, the sound they wish to produce (if they failed to do so they could not sing at all), they begin to think of their breath, their posture, their tongue and lips, the impression they are making upon their listeners and whatever else may happen to enter their minds at the moment.

Such haphazard thinking may not affect an artist adversely who has trained himself sufficiently to concentrate on the sound image. In a student, however, it is almost certain to produce many undesirable symptoms of the tension discussed above. If pursued unchecked for a long period of time, it may likewise be responsible for a paralyzing self-consciousness and stage fright.

I doubt if any beginner can manage to concentrate totally on a sound image for more than a few seconds at a time. After a while, however, if one happens to have a good ear and perseveres in trying, one could learn to concentrate in this fashion for longer periods of time. Eventually one can reach a stage of self-discipline where such concentration becomes nearly automatic and almost subconscious.

Mental image of a sound must, of course, include a most precise mental image of the vowel sound the singer intends to sing. Unless he can learn to hear mentally the vowel as precisely as he learns to hear the pitches and the rhythms he will be forced to resort to "mouthing" or to producing these vowels mechanically by means of direct muscular effort. This, of course, will nullify all that he might have gained in freedom of production by learning to concentrate on the image of the pitch of a sound.

It seems to me that every student must try his very utmost to experiment with himself to find the ways and means of attaining and perfecting this ability to concentrate. Little, if any, practical advice can be given on how to proceed in attaining such concentration. Each individual must find pro-

57

cedures suitable to him. I should imagine that singing a series of slow, sustained pitches on one vowel would serve nicely as an elementary exercise in continuous concentration on the sound image.

The student must also bear in mind the fact that there seems to be a definite relationship between his ability to concentrate on the mental image of a sound and his ability to relax while singing.

"Relaxation," insofar as the term is used in singing, does not, of course, imply the simultaneous relaxation of all the voluntary muscles of the body. It denotes a manner of singing where all the muscles remain in a normal, minimally flexed state, excepting those which are indispensable to the production of a sound, and such concurrent activities as standing, walking, etc. It is very difficult if not impossible to attain such an equilibrium of activity by direct volition or by direct muscular control. To say to oneself, "Relax this or that set of muscles while singing," for instance, will almost invariably produce added tension in these very muscles because, in this way, one would rivet one's attention to their activity. When, however, a student learns to concentrate to the utmost on the mental image of the sound he wishes to produce and has, therefore, no opportunity to think of himself and of the workings of his body, the possibility of avoiding unnecessary tension is greatly increased.

The relationship between the degree of concentration on the mental sound image and the effect such concentration has upon one's ability to relax is best illustrated when one considers the fact that certain types of tremolo or "wobble" due to overtenseness can sometimes be completely eliminated as soon as the singer learns really to concentrate on the image of the sustained sound he wishes to produce for its full duration.

One could attempt to formulate the foregoing in some such manner as:

1—The greater the singer's concentration on the complete sound image, the more relaxed his body seems to become.

2—The more the singer tries to concentrate on the muscular activities involved in his singing, the more tense these very muscles he is trying to control may become.

3—The more the singer's mind wanders during singing, appraising and analyzing the manner in which he is singing, the more self-conscious and tense he is likely to become.

The manner in which most students of singing try to solve the problem of singing rapid florid passages offers another excellent example of how this same type of misconception concerning the nature of the singer's instrument affects one's vocal technic.

Most students seem to believe that the ability to sing accurately a series of rapidly changing pitches is synonymous with a superior muscular skill. To develop this muscular skill or "flexibility" of their vocal apparatus, they often resort to a great number of gymnastic exercises especially designed for such a purpose. In so doing, they again try unsuccessfully to adopt the procedure an instrumentalist uses in solving a similar problem. The speed with which an instrumentalist can produce a series of changing pitches does depend to an enormous degree upon his ability to control directly and gymnastically the muscles responsible for the production of such pitches. This is especially true where keyboard instruments are concerned. The initial stages of acquiring such speed are, in instrumental playing, purely mechanical; a gymnastic exercising of his fingers is the first step toward acquiring any degree of automatic coordination between his inner ear and his muscles. As a matter of fact, a keyboard instrumentalist can learn to produce pitches rapidly and with great accuracy without involving his inner ear in the process.

We know, however, that no direct control is possible over those muscles the contraction of which determines the pitch of a sound produced by a human voice. The control of such muscles can only be attained by forming a precise mental image of the pitch. A singer must, therefore, learn to imagine pitches at the speed he wishes to sing them before he can hope to acquire any facility in producing such pitches. There is no such thing as a flexible or inflexible voice unless one chooses so to designate some rare pathological abnormality. There is, however, such a thing as a flexible or an inflexible musical ear. Those of us who possess a good musical ear can train it to become so flexible (that is, to imagine accurate pitches so rapidly) that the voice will be compelled to follow suit. Those, however, whose musical ear is only average or below average will not be able to train it to imagine a series of rapidly changing pitches clearly enough to compel their voices to reproduce these pitches. No singer can learn to sing faster than he can imagine pitches. Practically every instrumentalist, however, can learn to play faster than he can hear mentally if he so chooses.

It seems to me that too many voice students waste a great deal of time and energy in trying to limber up their voices without first trying to limber up their ability to imagine pitches.

Many students, if not most, would benefit, in my opinion, if they would endeavor really to learn to hear the florid passages they are trying to sing before they attempt to perform them. Insufficient musical preparation is almost invariably responsible for the so-called lack of flexibility of one's voice, that is, provided the natural musical ear of the singer is sufficiently keen to begin with. The often-expressed idea that heavy and low voices lack natural muscular flexibility is not supported by facts. Any type of voice is capable of singing coloratura passages, but not every singer possesses a sufficiently keen ear to do so, nor, if possessing a good enough ear, uses it intelligently enough to allow his voice to do so. We could not otherwise explain the fact that some basses, for instance, can sing rapid florid passages with more ease and accuracy than many a coloratura soprano. An intelligent approach to the study of florid music could be outlined in some such fashion as the following:

1—Learn to play the florid passage slowly and in rhythm.
2—Check each interval in your mind until the pattern of the passage is clearly established in your mind.
3—Without playing, try to hear as much of the passage as you can mentally, looking at it. Check spots where you are unsure of the intonation by playing them on the piano. Do it very slowly but in time, preferably with a metronome.
4—Gradually increase the tempo in which you mentally hear the passage. Remember that unless you can hear it mentally at the speed you imagine it must go, you will not be able to sing it. Do not attempt to sing it until you can hear it mentally at MM ♩ 76 if it is composed of sixteenths or at MM ♩ 92 if it is composed of triplet eighths. (If it is composed of thirty-seconds, or triplet sixteenths, use ♪ 76 and ♪ 92 speed.)
5—Learn to renew mentally the image of the vowel sound with each change of pitch. This is not to be confused with "aspiration" or with inserting an "h" between the pitches,

which is a most annoying mannerism. If you can only learn to hear the change of pitches but neglect to hear the vowel anew with each pitch, you will not accomplish much. Doing so, you will become very tense trying to maintain the vowel sound by muscular effort while attempting to sing the pitches under the guidance of your ear.

6—Avoid violent accentuation on each group of three or four notes comprising the unit of a ♩ or an ♪. It is sufficient to feel the rhythmic pulse; too strong an accent on the first note of each unit may create an unnecessary tension within your voice.

7—Sing the run very slowly when you have reached the stage at which you can hear it mentally at a fair speed. Check vowel, intonation and accentuation most carefully.

8—When you can hear the run clearly in your own mind at the speed at which it ought to go in your opinion, sing it several times at half this speed.

9—Hear it mentally accurately at slightly faster speed than the one you believe is required of you. When this is accomplished, you may be sufficiently well prepared to begin to practice it at the speed you want.

It seems to me that much of vocalization, especially rapid vocalization (in which scale and triad patterns are used as a rule), does considerable damage to the singer's ear. Constantly shifting the key in which he sings (C major, D flat major, D major, etc.) tends to disturb the clear image of the key center of a scale and a triad. It would help many singers to learn to vocalize in each key for a few minutes so that the interval relationship in each key is properly established. The continuous shifting of key center by semitones tends to make most students' intonation slovenly.

The habit of sliding or "scooping" is another undesirable feature of singing caused by insufficient accuracy in forming a mental image of sound.

A singer who cannot sing two sounds in succession without sliding between them is simply unable to form in his mind a rhythmically precise image of these two sounds. He is obviously unable to make up his mind when, precisely, to stop singing one and to begin to sing the other. This terribly slovenly habit is often honored by calling it legato, as if legato were an excuse for singing each note off pitch for a fraction of its duration. The student must remember that the habit of forming a rhythmically precise image of a sound in which pitch and vowel are combined is as important as the habit of forming a precise image of its pitch and its vowel.

A specified time is supposed to be occupied by a specified pitch and a specified vowel. If this pitch or vowel is initially inaccurate, yet becomes accurate sometime later, it proves that the singer has not conceived accurately the time at which he was supposed to attack the required pitch and the vowel.

Practically every aspect of singing and speaking is affected to a greater or lesser degree by the clarity of the mental image of the sound the singer or speaker wishes to produce. The coordination of muscular activities, for instance, necessary for the production of an accurate vowel sound depends to a very considerable degree upon the formation of a precise image of the vowel. Precise lip and tongue movement does not automatically result in the production of an equally precise vowel sound, if the image of this vowel is not clear in the mind of the speaker or singer. Many American students, for instance, often vainly try to produce a French "u" vowel by pushing their lips out until they look like members of the Ubangi tribe. Because they simply neglect to take the trouble to try to imagine what a French "u" sounds like and rely only on the direct conscious control of their tongue and lips, they fail to produce an accurate enough vowel notwithstanding all their efforts. The formation of a precise sound image in one's mind unifies and directs the innumerable and minute series of muscular contractions necessary for its production. True, it is possible to control one's lips and tongue by direct conscious effort; yet the delicate gauging of distances and tensions necessary for the production of a clear and accurate vowel is so minute that an inaccurate sound may just as easily be produced if one relies solely on such direct control. A person, however, who knows the sound by ear may contort his lips and tongue in a most unorthodox fashion and yet be able to produce the precise sound. Much of the tension and discomfort in singing is caused by a neglect of this principle. Many voice students seem not to begrudge the time and effort spent in consciously forcing their tongues, lips and jaws into some so-called "proper vowel position" and thus adding considerable and unnecessary tension to their singing; this same amount of effort spent on trying to form a clear image of the vowel sound they wish to sing would produce far more desirable results in an overwhelming majority of cases.

Almost the only aspect of singing and speaking where precise mechanical action may seem desirable and where precise knowledge of the muscular processes involved may be of some practical value, is in the production of consonants. Consonants are executed by the action of either the tongue or the lips, for all practical purposes unaided. The knowledge of the fact, therefore, that consonants like *l, n, d, t, r* are produced by the action of the tip of the tongue only and that they do not necessitate any perceptible closure of the mouth or any action of the part of the lips, may prove of great help to a singer who unnecessarily involves his entire sound-producing apparatus in their execution. The knowledge of such simple facts is easy to obtain. Practically every high school textbook on speech or phonetics describes in a most precise and helpful manner the muscular processes involved in the production of consonants. Most singers would profit greatly by drilling their tongue and lips in the same manner as an instrumentalist drills his fingers, but only where consonant production is involved. Such an approach will not prove equally helpful where the production of vowels is concerned. As discussed before, it will not prove of value if accepted as applicable to almost all other phases of studying singing.

The same general principle, namely that direct conscious control of one's muscles may prove to be inadequate if used without some unifying idea of its aim, holds true to a considerable degree even where any pattern of normal activity of voluntary muscles is concerned. When we pick up a piece of paper from the floor, we do not concern ourselves with the innumerable series of muscular contractions involved in the process. Our only concern is with the aim of these extraordinarily complex muscular activities. Let us suppose that, instead of saying "pick up this piece of paper from the floor," we should attempt to describe the muscular activities involved; 1) in bending down, 2) bending the knees, 3) stretching the arm, 4) grasping the paper with the fingers, 5) retracting the arm, 6) straightening the knees, 7) straightening the back, etc.

To do so precisely and in clearly stated detail would, no doubt, require more pages than this little book contains. The measurements of distances would have to be precise to the hundredth of an inch, the measurements of energy demanded would involve most complicated calculations. The net result might, and probably would, be that the person following these extremely precise instructions but not given a unifying idea of the *aim* of the muscular actions demanded of him, would not be able to pick up the piece of paper from the floor. He probably would, in the process of just trying to flex his muscles in such a precise manner, come very near to a general coordinatory breakdown.

Any and every one of our most trivial actions necessitates the coordination of hundreds of series of complex muscular contractions. The most exact knowledge of such processes does not, in itself, help a normal person to coordinate any more easily or efficiently. We learn to coordinate from the moment that we are born, not by learning to analyze which muscles we flex and how we flex them, but by trying to attain a variety of different aims such as grabbing the toy in front of us, crawling toward some objective or imitating the sounds that we hear.

Even so, I do not minimize the value of practical advice on certain specific matters concerning our muscular coordination. Expert, matter-of-fact advice on how to do something in an easy and efficient manner can be of great value; but I fail to see how anyone who possesses any natural aptitude for singing can be helped by being made conscious of all the complex physiological processes which are supposed to take place while he emits a sound. Even if the knowledge of such processes were accurate (which, as yet, is a very moot question), the consciousness of these minute physiological details would only tend to make a normal singer more tense, uncomfortable and distracted. In other words, it would decrease his coordinatory efficiency.

Many students of singing, for instance, are extraordinarily preoccupied with the manner in which they breathe. Sometimes this preoccupation almost reaches a maniacal stage. Breathing is a perfectly normal process, without a reasonably efficient functioning of it we cannot live, much less speak or sing. The preoccupation with the physiology of breathing makes the student so conscious of the muscular contractions involved that he is likely to lose most of his natural coordinatory control over it. It is obvious that efficient control of breathing is necessary for efficient singing. Most students, however, naturally possess the control necessary for their immediate needs. I should venture to suggest that if the needs for such control were gradually and carefully increased, a fairly gifted, physically normal student would gradually and rather easily find means to fulfill such demands with very little prompting. Made too conscious of some special manner of breathing at the very beginning of their studies, many students are never able to attain a normal coordination between the demands of their phrase and the control of breath necessary for its execution. Unconsciously, we exercise such coordinatory control constantly in our speech. It does not seem unreasonable to assume that it could serve as a basis upon which a singer's control over his breathing could be based.

Many students who have difficulty in controlling their breath would do well to remember that much of the time, for instance, they inhale more air than is needed for the phrase they are going to sing. Filled almost beyond their normal capacity, they become extremely tense trying to hoard this air within them. It seems natural that, under such conditions, little if any efficient control could be exercised over the emission of this air.

Much the same reasoning applies to the control of resonances we employ in singing. Any normal person employs unconsciously various resonances in his speech (such as chest resonance, nasal resonance etc.). The choice of resonances employed in singing should be based on those resonances which tend to make the use of one's speaking voice most efficient and effortless. Most vocal students would do well to try to learn how to speak clearly, rather loudly, not nasally and for long periods of time without tiring or becoming hoarse. The type of resonances employed in such speaking could then easily form the basis of the resonances used in their singing. Any conscious muscular effort designed to produce automatically the desired resonance may, however, not result in its efficient or free use. The mechanical manipulation of resonances is one of the reasons for the extraordinarily inexpressive manner of singing which is so prevalent among students. Singing is then completely divorced from speaking, and the sound of the voice becomes artificial and meaningless. Because words are used in singing, it is one of the most directly communicative forms of musical art. To sacrifice the normal speaking resonance in search of some hypothetically perfect singing resonance which produces tone as opposed to speech instead of in conjunction with speech is perhaps one of the most self-contradictory practices, for every student tries to be expressive without realizing that much of his practicing may be directed at incapacitating his most valuable tool of expression, his normal speech.

We now come to what is perhaps the most controversial part of our discussion. It concerns itself with the question of perfectability of the vocal mechanism as such.

A violinist who happens to possess an inferior, factory-made instrument will not try to rebuild it into a Stradivarius as he knows full well that such a feat is impossible. He will endeavor to buy, borrow, beg or steal an instrument which he deems adequate for his purposes. A singer, however, cannot exchange his voice for another one. It is only natural that he, therefore, seeks ways and means to improve his voice as such, and not only to improve the manner in which he uses it.

68

Besides, a young singer's instrument is neither fully developed physically, nor are its possibilities fully explored. It may, and often does, change considerably before he reaches full maturity. The controversial issue is: Can proper exercise develop an inferior instrument beyond its natural capacity, that is, change its basic quality, extend its range and increase its volume?

Those who claim that voices can be "rebuilt" cite examples of great singers whose voices at the outset of their careers were considered by experts to be inferior. Those who claim that no one can rebuild an inferior voice into a superior instrument counter that the men and women cited as examples of such rebuilding always did possess the great voices for which they later became justly famous, but that they used them so poorly at the beginning as to disguise completely their natural quality, range and volume. I incline to favor the latter point of view. It seems to me that if the voice is used efficiently (that is, guided by one's ear and reasonably free of unnecessary muscular tension), little, if anything, can be done to improve its quality and increase its range and volume by exercise, especially if the voice in question happens to be mature.

It is true that spectacular changes occur sometimes in the timbre, range and volume of a voice during several years of study. Such changes, however, cannot be honestly attributed to some physical alterations of the structure of a vocal apparatus induced by exercises. The physical structure of the vocal apparatus remains virtually unchanged after it reaches full maturity and until it begins to deteriorate with very advanced age. Of course, it happens rather frequently that the stage of physical maturity is reached during the years a singer studies most intensively. The physiological changes which may occur during this time cannot, therefore, be credited to exercise and study. More efficient, musical and confident use of a voice, however, can, and often does, make it sound far better than it may have sounded when it was used inefficiently, unmusically and timidly. The fact that an excellent voice may be so poorly handled as to appear inadequate does not at all mean that an inadequate voice can be handled so well as to appear excellent.

"Building" a voice, that is, attempting to endow it with a quality, range and volume it does not seem to possess naturally, results, more often than not, in making the student lose control of whatever limited range and volume and whatever mediocre quality he may have had. Attempts at forcible extension of range and volume can, and often do, result in severe physical damage to the vocal cords due to overstrain, especially if pursued relentlessly and with conviction by both student and teacher. Attempts at forcible acquisition of some rare timbre which the voice of some extraordinarily gifted singer may possess can, and often do, result in severe musical and artistic damage to the student. This is especially true when such attempts are based on the belief that such a rare timbre is not natural, but is only due to some type of acquirable skill with which the singer uses his voice.

Sometimes a rare high voice has the quality which is similar in its timbre to a low voice. Such quality is unusual and makes the voice an instrument out of the ordinary. Such quality can no more be acquired by exercise than can remarkable and unusually beautiful facial features. Too many tenors and sopranos try to make the timbre of their voices sound like Caruso's or Ponselle's. They conveniently forget that could Caruso's or Ponselle's timbre be imitated successfully at will, neither voice could have been considered such an utterly extraordinary instrument.

I happened to notice an advertisement once which ran as

follows: 'WHY ENVY A BEAUTIFUL VOICE, HAVE ONE'. This advertisement is, perhaps, the most perfect expression of the attitude of those who believe, or pretend to believe, in the possibility of changing an average voice into a superior one by directed exercise. In practically no other field of study could such an attitude take as firm a root as it has in singing. In no other field of study does it reap such rich rewards. No college has yet advertised: "Why envy a scientist's brain, have one." No physical culture school has dangled in front of its students the slogan: "Why envy a heavyweight, be one." Not even beauty shops and "success schools" dare to go that far in the description of wonders they will perform for those who are willing to pay the required fee.

In discussing ear training, I stated rather categorically that no student whose natural ear is poor can expect the study of ear training to equip him with an equivalent of a good musical ear. Now I am forced to repeat just as categorically that no more or less mature student whose voice is naturally mediocre in quality, range and volume can expect the study of vocal technic to equip him with an equivalent of a superior natural voice. It is true that if one possesses an unusually good musical ear, considerable talent and intelligence above the average, one can learn, under proper guidance, how to use whatever voice one happens to have to the best possible advantage. No one can expect the study of vocal technic to do more than just that. I must repeat again that, in my experience, I have found that too many serious voice students look upon the study of vocal technic as a way of acquiring what nature has denied them.

I should like to sum up my attitude toward the subject of "voice building" as follows: If a more or less mature student sings very inefficiently, tensely and unmusically, he can be helped to sing more efficiently, freely and musically provided he has a good ear and some musical feeling. This may have a marked effect upon the quality, range and volume of his voice. If his voice happens to be superior, the change in its quality, range and volume will then be remarkable. If his voice happens to be average, the change will be very noticeable, but the inherent limitations of his voice will not be eradicated. If his voice happens to be poor, the change effected by the efficient and musical use of it may be very noticeable to the singer, but will be of little value to his listeners.

It seems to me that one of the most important considerations in approaching the study of vocal technic is a clear-cut distinction between the singer's skill and his instrument. The effect that skilled use has upon the structure of the instrument as such, physiologically speaking, is negligible. Lack of skill, however, may make a superior instrument sound inadequate. Such utter lack of skill, though, is very rarely encountered among gifted beginners. If encountered, it usually is of neurotic origin. Such lack of skill is most frequently found among students who have average voices, average talent and have studied unintelligently, or among such beginners who simply have too little of everything.

In conjunction with this, I would like to make a few remarks concerning the educational methods sometimes employed in the teaching of singers. Some of such methods rest upon the premise that only by trying to do things too difficult for him at the moment can a student *develop* his voice and improve the manner in which he uses it. I cannot agree with the idea that in order to learn to do an easy thing well, a singer must learn to do a difficult thing badly. Because of the apparent prevalence of this idea, many singers try to sing music which demands vocal powers which they either do not possess at all, or do not as yet possess. Learning to strain through songs and arias beyond one's immediate physical capacity accomplishes only the following: 1) It makes the student feel the immediate inadequacy of his voice very acutely. This feeling of inadequacy increases the tension with which he sings. The increase of tension affects adversely his entire singing. 2) It also creates within the student a number of unpleasant, deeply ingrained associations, almost phobias, which this piece of music evokes automatically every time he is confronted with it.

The effect such associations have on his singing is often extremely undesirable. It often makes it impossible for him ever to manage to perform adequately the piece of music used for such educational experiments. He may not be able to sing it well even when his voice and the skill with which he uses it have reached the point of development where a piece of this sort should no longer present any difficulties for him. Since mostly very celebrated arias and songs are used in this capacity of "guinea pig" pieces, many a singer, when he finally reaches a full realization of his powers, sees himself revert involuntarily to the inadequate singing of his student days every time he has to perform such a piece. Unfortunately he may have to perform them very frequently. I am willing to admit that the student may develop a sort of endurance under such training. However, it seems to me that endurance can be equally well acquired in a less hazardous manner. It seems rather unnecessary to jeopardize one's singing for the sake of learning how to endure making loud noises for long periods of time.

I do not see why a student cannot learn to sing beautifully within the range in which he can operate with reasonable freedom before he attempts to extend his range any further. Most students who have been educated by means of

73

attempting the impossible simply become rigid with fear and worry when they have to sing above the stave. I believe that had they been taught to sing within the stave easily, efficiently and musically, they could gradually and without much difficulty extend the range of their voice to its full natural capacity. I do not see why a student cannot learn to sing beautifully between mezzo-piano and mezzo-forte before he begins to try to sing fortissimo. I fail to see how one can learn to sing very loudly if one's vocal apparatus is, at the moment, incapable of producing such volume. I do not see how a singer can improve his voice or the manner in which he uses it if he demands from it certain physical characteristics which it may not possess either temporarily or permanently.

The volume and the pitch range of which each individual voice is capable are primarily determined by its type, its maturity and secondarily by the skill with which it is being used. A light soprano's middle C, sung forte, for instance, will never equal in volume the same pitch sung forte by an alto, any more than a forte middle C produced on a flute will equal in volume a forte middle C produced on a trombone.

Not many students seem to realize that each type of voice and each individual voice possesses its own dynamic range, just as much as it possesses its own pitch range and its own timbre. No absolute requirements of volume and range can be indiscriminately set up, but must at all times be considered in relation to the individual voice in question. Nothing seems quite as pitiful as an immature light soprano "developing" her voice by singing the parts of Tosca or Aida, or a baritone who cannot quite reach an E comfortably, singing Figaro in *The Barber of Seville* in order to "improve his range."

V. The Vocal Student and the Teaching of Vocal Technic

The procedures employed in the teaching of vocal technic are so many and so varied that even a most cursory description of those most frequently encountered would fill a very large volume. The concepts or approaches, however, upon which most procedures employed in the teaching of vocal technic seem to be based fall into four main categories.

The approach which I should like to discuss first may be termed mechanistic or if one wishes, scientific. This concept rests largely upon the following assumptions: 1) That accurate reproduction of certain physical conditions which have been observed during the emission of any desirable sound will automatically produce this desirable sound. 2) That the assimilation of accurate knowledge of physiological processes involved in the production of a desirable sound will enable the student to reproduce accurately such processes at will, thus reproducing the sound at will.

The teaching of vocal technic in this fashion rests primarily upon the teacher's knowledge of the physiology of singing or, as it sometimes happens, upon his knowledge of some singular lore which often employs physiological nomenclature.

I have argued at length against such mechanistic or scientific approach to the study of vocal technic. I fail to see how the most accurate knowledge of physiological processes involved in the production of a sound can enable one to reproduce such processes at will and so accurately as to allow one to produce the identical sound. In my opinion, all educational procedures resting upon that theory or any similar approach to the study of vocal technic can be dismissed as not valid.

Such training tends to impair a student's natural coordination, destroys whatever musicality he may possess, tends to promote the most sterile kind of self-analysis, and usually results in an abnormally self-conscious and, because of this, inefficient manner of singing.

If a scientifically accurate knowledge of the physiology of singing is used as a basis in any such teaching, the student's vocal apparatus will suffer no obvious physical damage. When, however, a poorly digested physiological terminology forms the sole basis of such an approach to the teaching of vocal technic, as unfortunately often happens, severe physical damage to the vocal apparatus of the student may be the result of such training.

It is true that a considerable body of scientifically acceptable data concerning the physiology of a human sound-producing apparatus has been assembled since the invention of the laryngoscope and other similar instruments. This data, however, has not yet been correlated with either the aesthetics or acoustics of singing nor with its psychology or its pedagogics. Our knowledge of the psychological processes involved in singing and in the teaching of singing is as yet simply inadequate. We may know accurately enough the positions assumed by the vocal cords, the uvula, the tongue and the other muscles while an aesthetically desirable sound of specified pitch and vowel is being produced. But this knowledge cannot enable a student to compel his vocal apparatus to assume this position so accurately as to produce a like sound.

The attitude held by many students that vocal technic is a discipline of knowledge which can be reasonably successfully acquired once certain detailed physiological information has been assimilated seems to me to be totally unwarranted. As unsatisfactory as this conclusion may seem to one in search of a scientific or mechanistic vocal technic, it is the only conclusion which seems to be supported by the available evidence.

Too many students clamor for an approach to vocal technic which in its crude mechanistic simplicity could not even help one to learn the finer points of plumbing. Such students must remember that they are not automobiles but people, with all the indescribable complexity of being a person implied. They either do not know or do not wish to know that vocal technic is inextricably connected with innumerable musical, emotional and intellectual factors which exercise an enormous influence upon the physiology of singing as well as upon the acoustic properties of vocalized sound.

This is often best demonstrated when the inability of a student to manage some certain passage without undue strain is corrected by directing his attention to rhythm, phrasing, dynamics and poetic content of this passage. When all these matters are assimilated, the purely physiological strain of production often disappears without even having been mentioned. The process of singing is then accompanied by a very comfortable sensation; yet, as often as not, the student searches again for some mechanical way to induce himself to experience anew this sensation which "feels right." As a rule he is unwilling to consider the fact that it was concentration on rhythm, phrasing, dynamics and poetic content which had enabled him to experience this freedom of production.

77

A student of singing must never forget that doing the physically "right thing," insofar as any so-called "method of production" is concerned, means absolutely nothing to anyone except the originator or the follower of any such method.

Much too often, the physically "right thing" is done to perfection while the result is unmusical, clumsy singing, a tormented sound, mechanical delivery and embarrassing self-consciousness; the disconcerting thing is that this sometimes happens to students who have some voice and some talent. Had they concerned themselves less with achieving the physiologically "correct production" and allowed themselves to make music and recite the words, they could have managed to sing at least acceptably, if not beautifully.

No one is interested in what manner a singer's throat, diaphragm, jaw and whatnot operate, except some few students and voice specialists who have forgotten that a singer is, after all, a performer and not a laboratory guinea pig. The rest of humanity judges a singer by the aural impact his singing makes upon them, caring not a fig whether he opens his mouth in accordance with "method x" or "method z," or tries to contract his larynx in accordance with "method y."

Since the invention of the laryngoscope, some teaching of vocal technic has assumed a "scientific" attitude which is, as yet, totally unwarranted by the extent of our knowledge. The scientific information at our disposal today is as insufficient for our understanding of the factors which govern the immensely complex operation of our sound-producing apparatus as the caloric theory was once insufficient for our understanding of nutrition. Perhaps it may not be impossible at some later date to teach people how to control their intellect, emotion, ability to imagine sounds, or even how to control directly the muscles of their sound-producing apparatus. At present, it seems presumptuous to approach the study of vocal technic with such an attitude, especially if this study is supposed to result in artistically valid singing. It is true that certain pathological conditions affecting the basic mechanics of our speech have been explored to some extent both physiologically and psychologically. It is equally true that certain methods have been devised by the use of which the mechanics of producing minimally efficient speech sounds can now be taught to deaf mutes, sufferers from cerebral palsy and others physically handicapped. Yet the knowledge which allows us to devise such procedures with success obviously cannot be of much practical value to one who is studying vocal technic in the hope of becoming a professional singer.

If we could ever reach a stage of such minute self-knowledge as to be able to teach singing in a truly scientific manner, singing as we know it would lose its purpose and its function, for singing, like all art, is a form of communication of matters which cannot be communicated successfully by any other known means. Should we ever learn so much about our intellect and our emotions as to be able to control them fully; should we ever learn so much about the relationship of such control to the control of our bodies; and should we ever devise a precise terminology for all of such processes, relationships and interrelationships, we would lose all need for the literary arts and, indirectly, for singing. An entirely new form of art would then arise, an art based on the scientifically perfect knowledge of what association produces what reaction in a human being. In such art only would successful assimilation of accurate knowledge become synonymous with the ability to employ this knowledge successfully in performance.

Another approach to the problem of teaching vocal technic rests largely on the assumptions that: 1) The singer cannot hear himself sing as others hear him, 2) Every sound is ac-

79

companied by a definite sensation within the singer's body, and 3) By teaching him how to experience a sensation which, in the opinion of the teacher, should accompany the production of a desired sound, one can teach him to produce the desired sound.

In any educational procedure designed to teach vocal technic and based on this approach to the problem, the question of semantics or the meanings of words is of paramount importance. We possess no standardized terminology designed for the purpose of describing the sensations caused by or accompanying the production of sound. In describing such matters, we are forced to use words of which there seem to be no general agreement as to meaning. Often the same word has different and even opposite meanings when used by different people.

There is nothing surprising in our inability to describe accurately the sensations produced within us by singing a sound. Our sensations are incommunicable as such unless we devise some adequate scale of references to which we could compare them. Sensations of taste, smell, sight, sound and touch are impossible to communicate as such unless the other person has already experienced such sensations and can remember, compare and imagine them. Can one accurately describe the touch of velvet to one who has never felt velvet or a similar fabric, or the smell of cooked cabbage to one who has never smelled cooked cabbage? Can one accurately describe the shade of a color to one who has never seen its equivalent, or the sound of a trombone to one who has never heard a brass instrument played? How then can we describe a sensation caused within our body by the emission of a middle C?

The only possible way even to try to communicate the "feel" of a sensation is by employing either a simile or a metaphor. Metaphor is defined in most dictionaries as "a figure of speech in which a likeness is attributed or comparison made by putting one object or idea for another." The degree of effectiveness with which we can devise metaphors or similes to describe a sensation is, in the end, determined by the degree of literary talent or skill one happens to have. Teaching vocal technic in such fashion obviously would require some degree of poetic or literary talent on the part of the teacher. The unfortunate fact is, of course, that most teachers of vocal technic are, as a rule, very inept poets and that their use of such literary devices is often extremely reckless and misleading. It often happens that instead of communicating the "feel" of some sensation to the student, they often influence him to attempt the physically impossible.

A famous singer and voice teacher used, for instance, the following image when teaching a student to approach a high note: "Sink your nose into your larynx when attacking this note." Such a statement is, of course, pure fancy. If taken to imply that it describes a certain definite action by which one could sink one's nose into one's larynx, it would indicate the belief that such an extraordinary feat could actually take place. The student who would repeatedly attempt to achieve such a contortion would surely land either in an insane asylum or a hospital; but those who understood this advice could conceivably profit by it for what it was, an effort to influence the student indirectly, almost "poetically" (if one could term such an image as poetry). Another equally prominent singer and teacher used to advise students to "sink through the floor" on a high note, another to "fly through the air," another to "feel the breath in the knees," another to "shape the throat like a pear."

When such flamboyant imagery is mixed with a pseudo-scientific physiological jargon, and when the "feel as if" injunction is interpreted by the student to mean "do such and

81

such," the whole procedure reaches the stage of a grotesque farce. Then students try actually to shape their throats like pears, take a breath with their knees, sing through the backs of their heads and generally attempt feats of such a prodigious nature that, could they ever succeed in executing any of them successfully, they would surely achieve great fame, at least among the medical profession.

The extraordinary flights of fancy of which some teachers of vocal technic are capable would put to shame the most fantastically-minded surrealist poet. Many a studio much of the time is filled with such exhortations as: "feel as if the tone is elliptical and is arched between your diaphragm and the top of your head," "see your tone wedged between your teeth," or "rolling on the floor" or "bobbing behind your eyes," "feel soap bubbles rising in your throat," "feel as if your throat were on the top of your skull." If such attempts at communication are very "poetic," that is flowery and unintelligible, they do no particular harm. If, however, they deal with larynges, pharynges, vocal cords, tongues and diaphragms, they might have even more undesirable effect upon the student than has the more scientific training. Unless used by one who has a great poetic gift, they have, as a rule, little effect altogether except to make an average beginner who is not used to that sort of thing very uncomfortable.

All three assumptions on which this approach to the teaching of vocal technic is based are, in my opinion, completely valid. The trouble lies in the oversight of the fact that we possess no means to communicate a sensation. If we did, this approach to the teaching of vocal technic would be most effective and most helpful. It is not inconceivable for some extraordinarily gifted teacher to employ such a procedure with good results, particularly in the teaching of a very gifted student, and especially if it is used in conjunction with the "trial and error" approach which will be discussed later.

Semantic insecurity affects to a greater or lesser degree all procedures employed in the teaching of vocal technic. Not only are we unable to describe accurately the sensations accompanying the emission of a sound, but we have no generally acceptable terminology designed to describe the properties of a sound produced by a human voice.

Certain properties of sound produced by a human voice are communicable. We have words designed to describe such properties on the meaning of which a general agreement seems to exist. Such words are very few indeed; they deal with the pitch and duration of a sound and, to a lesser degree, with its volume, with the vowel employed in its production, with the type of voice a person happens to possess (such as bass, tenor, soprano), and possibly with some obvious resonances employed in the production of a sound (such as chest resonance, nasal resonance, falsetto). Any other characteristic of a sound must be described by words designed for other purposes such as, for instance, "liquid," "dry," "warm," "cold," etc.

These words, when used to describe the quality or qualities of a sound, are endowed with an arbitrary, private code meaning of the user. No amount of further verbal explanation can communicate such code meaning. To be able to understand it, one must learn to associate sound varieties with the code names given to them by the inventor of that particular code and under his guidance, for it stands to reason that the quality called "liquid" by A can, with equal justification, be called "dry" by B. One must also have absolute trust in the reliability of the ear of the inventor of such a code, for it is obvious that unless A can identify unerringly every time that quality which he calls "liquid," or B can do likewise with the quality he calls "dry," the very core of the code meaning with which these words are endowed by A and B becomes too vague to be followed by anyone else.

Until the aesthetics and the acoustics of singing have been correlated, that is, until the acoustic properties of a sound designated as "liquid" by one person and "dry" by another have been agreed upon, singer, critic, teacher and student will not be able to communicate freely with one another. This absence of any reliable nomenclature is, perhaps, responsible for the extraordinary diversity of opinion among singers, critics and teachers concerning the manner in which a student can be trained to produce sounds considered desirable. It is very seldom that the description of sound as such is used in discussing singing, inadequate as such description may be. Most of the time such a description is accompanied by attempts to describe also the manner in which the listener imagines the sound has been produced. Likewise, it is often accompanied by an attempt to describe the sensation which, in the opinion of the listener, the singer must have experienced while producing the sound.

This, of course, adds immeasurably to the semantic confusion. A may call a certain sound "thick and closed" while B may call the same sound "spread and open"—and both with equal justification. It seems that the more explicit we try to be in discussing singing, the less intelligible we become.

Whether we ever shall be able to devise some sort of standardized nomenclature to be used in teaching and discussing vocal technic remains to be seen. It seems, however, that it would not be impossible to extend the range of a specially designed nomenclature beyond the utterly inadequate limits within which it is now confined.

Another procedure which is frequently employed in the teaching of vocal technic is based primarily on direct imitation. There is a great deal of common sense in this approach; it is perhaps the easiest way to acquaint the student with the type of sound the teacher considers desirable as well as with the manner of production considered desirable, something which cannot be done too easily, if at all, by verbal explanation. The main dangers of this procedure are: 1) The probability that the natural qualities of the teacher's and the student's voices are very different and that the student may try to imitate the quality of his teacher's voice—an artistically stultifying procedure which may have very undesirable effects on the student's singing. 2) The fact that each singer develops a number of mannerisms in his singing. These mannerisms are often due to the individual structure of the singer's vocal apparatus or to his mental and musical idiosyncrasies. Such mannerisms are often the most easily observable features of the teacher's singing and are often imitated by the students, since they seem to believe that by imitating such mannerisms they will also be able to imitate the features of the teacher's singing they most admire.

The idea that by imitating certain visible characteristics of a great singer, one may approximate the ease of production and the quality of the sound this singer may produce is one of the most widespread fallacies among vocal students. Seeing a famous singer twist his mouth in some special manner or stand in some certain way while he sings, these students dutifully attempt to imitate such mannerisms. They hope, of course, that should they only manage to do so, they could not fail to approximate the singing of an artist they admire.

Such reasoning is very similar to the primitive reasoning on which the belief in magic is based. In magic, cause and effect are considered interchangeable. A farcical *reductio ad absurdum* of such an attitude would admit that by growing a beard and taking to drink, one could become a great poet, since many a great poet was a drunkard and wore a beard.

We have, as yet, no way of establishing a clear distinction between: 1) factors which cause the sound to possess certain definite properties in general; 2) factors which cause the sound to possess certain definite properties if produced by a specific vocal apparatus possessing certain distinctive structural pecularities; 3) factors which are purely incidental and accompany the production of a sound (instead of causing it); and 4) factors which could be termed a form of involuntary, individual nervous reaction to the process of producing a sound.

Every singer discovers during his professional life, certain "tricks" or devices which, for some reason or another, seem to help him to do what he wishes to do. Such token action is often based on association patterns which are purely individual. As a rule, such devices are determined by the complex interrelationship between the singer's physique, talent, background, training and emotional and intellectual make-up. They work well with him often in a manner of some magic ceremonial which many of us seem to follow when, for instance, we carry lucky coins and rabbits' feet about us, or eat some special food or go through some special routine before important occasions.

Often, however, such tricks are due to some physical peculiarities the singer may possess. One can imagine a singer with a peculiarly formed mouth discover that by stretching his lips in some certain fashion he can make the production of certain high pitches of certain desired quality more easy and more assured for himself. If the student forgets to take into account the shape and size of such a singer's mouth, he may attempt to stretch his own lips in precisely the same manner while singing high notes. He will attempt to do so even though his own mouth may be so different in shape and structure that this action will well nigh incapacitate him; and yet, knowing that the great X does just that while singing the high notes for which he is so justly famous, the student will, as a rule, persist, believing that the fault lies only with the lack of precision with which he stretches his lips and believing that if he could only learn to reproduce this mannerism precisely enough, his own high notes will be bound to improve and to resemble those of X. This constant uncertainty in distinguishing the causes from the symptoms in singing perhaps makes the study of vocal technic such an elusive and personal process.

Teaching vocal technic by direct imitation would require an unusual degree of selfknowledge and objectivity on the part of the teacher, qualities which are extremely rare among all people and especially rare among performing artists.

Teaching vocal technic by direct imitation may have excellent results if: 1) the student and the teacher have very similar voices; 2) have similar backgrounds and personalities; 3) have a similar physique; 4) have a similar type of talent. In most other instances, it seems to work rather inadequately unless, as I mentioned before, the teacher has an extraordinarily lucid mind.

At this point, it seems only fair to add that these three approaches to the teaching of vocal technic are very seldom employed in their pure form. What happens most frequently is that the vocal teacher employs procedures based on all these approaches to the problem of teaching. As a rule, however, an average teacher leans heavily on some procedure based either on the mechanistic, the sensation or the direct imitation approach in trying to teach his student the elements of vocal technic. The more pronounced in one's teaching is the preference for some such basic philosophy, the more inflexible it becomes, and, in my opinion, the less realistic and the less effective.

The oldest and, I believe, the most sensible approach to the teaching of vocal technic is the one based on experimentation or trial and error. It is purely empiric and eclectic. Its motto could very well be: "Try anything; if it makes you sing comfortably and produce a good sound, it is right." It rests on the assumption that until the student has somehow or other managed to imagine a sound considered desirable by the teacher, the student cannot be expected either to produce this sound or to experience the sensations accompanying its production. The procedure on which this kind of teaching rests, presupposes constant experimentation by the student who is guided by the criticism of his teacher. Little verbal explanation is necessary in such teaching. The aesthetic judgment of the teacher, his familiarity with the psychological problems of singing and teaching, and his knowledge of what can and what cannot be directly controlled in a vocal apparatus serve as a basis on which such procedures can be successfully employed. An excellent ear, a very considerable familiarity with the type of sound a human voice can be expected to produce, a familiarity which cannot be acquired without extensive personal experience with all types of singers, an extensive aural knowledge of phonetics, a realistic appraisal of what an individual voice is capable of at the different stages of its physical development, great patience and an almost intuitive insight into the personality of the student are, of course, indispensable to such teaching.

It cannot adhere to any mechanistic dogma and it recognizes vocal technic for what it is—a way of singing developed by the student himself by experimentation and depending largely upon his natural ability. Because of this, such a procedure of teaching must, by necessity, take into account the individual traits of the student and always be pliable enough to employ any means which may seem practicable in the case of the individual student as well as discard any means which prove ineffective.

Under such training, the student has the best possible chance to develop gradually a manner of singing in which the mental image of a sound, the production of this sound and the sensation caused within his body by the production of this sound become coordinated and welded into a solid unit with which he can operate at will.

Let us sum up certain matters already discussed in the last two chapters:

1—A singer cannot hear himself sing as others hear him.
2—We have no adequate nomenclature to describe accurately the sound produced by a human voice.
3—We have no direct means to communicate a sensation accompanying the production of a sound.
4—We have no direct control over the muscles primarily responsible for the pitch and quality of sound we produce.
5—The primary control a singer possesses over his vocal apparatus is mental (due to the formation of a precise mental image of the sound he wishes to produce).
6—We have little if any knowledge of how this control can be learned by one who does not already possess it to some degree.
7—We have little if any scientific knowledge of how precisely this control operates.

8—The available evidence points to the fact that possession of accurate knowledge of physiological processes involved in singing does not enable one to reproduce such processes at will accurately enough.

Because of all this, it becomes obvious that one cannot, as yet, speak of vocal technic as of some generally acceptable discipline of knowledge. It would seem more sensible to speak of specific vocal technics or approaches to vocal technic as taught by X, Y and Z. In evaluating these, only the purely practical criterion is valid—does technic X help student A to sing?

The student must realize that the study of vocal technic is as yet one of the most elusive processes subject to the action and counteraction of a great number of intangibles. Of these intangibles we know as yet too little to be able to discuss them with authority.

One may form an idea of the complexity and variety of such intangibles if one considers that the success and failure of this study depends to an extraordinary degree on such matters as the personality of both student and teacher, their aesthetic preferences, their cultural backgrounds and their individual physical and mental idiosyncrasies (which influence their manner of singing and their approach to the study of singing). It depends equally on the degree of their sensitivity to music and to poetry, their skill with words, their psychological insight and on a multitude of other complex factors equally intangible and undefinable.

Teaching, as well as studying vocal technic could, therefore, be most accurately described as an art. The impersonal (or scientific) element in such teaching is, for all practical purposes, nonexistent. This should be clearly understood by anyone who is trying to study singing seriously.

It seems to me that, in view of all the intangibles involved in the study and teaching of singing, any theorizing on what is a right way and what is a wrong way of producing a sound can be reduced to the following formula: If the sound as such is acceptable to the teacher, the manner in which it may be produced is correct provided such a manner is comfortable to the student. If only the manner in which the sound is produced is unacceptable to the teacher but the sound itself is acceptable and the student feels comfortable, this manner ought to be considered as one suited to the student's needs. The total disregard by many teachers of the vocal technic of the sounds which their students emit, so long as they contort themselves in some approved fashion, is unfortunately very prevalent. The total disregard of the fact that any such approved manner of production may make some student extremely tense and uncomfortable while singing is also, unfortunately, very often encountered. Any theorizing as to what manner of production ought to be right is, after all, nothing but conjecture; it cannot as yet be supported by any scientifically incontrovertible array of facts.

It is customary to consider the study of vocal technic in terms of muscular processes of producing sound. Many seem to believe that efficiency in such muscular processes can be attained in a purely gymnastic fashion basing their belief on the assumption that since such a procedure is used in acquiring digital facility, it could be used with equally good results in acquiring vocal facility. In the foregoing pages, I have tried to point out that such an approach to the study of vocal technic is utterly unrealistic, since it neglects to take into account the importance of the nonmuscular factors which govern and coordinate the muscular activity of a vocalist. No vocalist can directly control most of the muscles of his sound-producing apparatus by gymnastics. He must gain control over the mental factors which coordinate, govern and direct their operation.

It seems to me, therefore, that the acquisition of vocal technic should primarily rest on the acquisition of control over the nonmuscular factors involved in singing. Efficiency in singing should rest on the technic of controlling such primary, causative factors of singing as one's ability to imagine sounds, and on the technic of controlling one's emotions and intellect. The degree to which a student can learn to control his body efficiently rests primarily on the degree to which he can learn to control his mind. In other words, I firmly believe that before a singer tries to train his body to be obedient he should try to train his mind to give commands which can be obeyed.

The belief that the study of vocal technic (conceived as a study of physical processes of producing sounds) is equal and synonymous with the study of singing is equally widespread. This mistaken identification of singing with vocal technic, and of vocal technic with direct muscular control, is so prevalent as to be almost generally accepted. This substitution of identities is perhaps due to the fact that nothing seems as comforting to us as the belief that some manner of study in which a certain definite mechanical action is supposed to produce automatically certain results can be applied to all human activity, including art.

Here perhaps lies the root of all mechanistic conceptions of singing, of all the singular "voice building" practices which one so often encounters, and of all the attitudes toward the study of singing which try to minimize the part that abundant natural endowment and talent play in the making of a singer.

Hence the emphasis on vocal technic, conceived as some

manner of direct control over the muscles of one's sound-producing apparatus, which manner of control, if "correct," can be attained regardless of the amount and quality of a student's nonmuscular equipment. Hence the attempt to identify the study of singing with the study of some such vocal technic.

However, vocal technic is, as yet, a rather vague and almost totally unsystematized field of study. In this field where neither the educational procedures nor the basic approaches upon which such procedures must rest, nor even the aims of such procedures are clearly defined and where no standardized terminology exists or where even the basic requirements for studying or teaching are almost impossible to formulate, anyone who can persuade any number of students that he is a teacher of vocal technic (used as a synonym for singing) can become a teacher of "singing."

It is not surprising, therefore, that a number of outright swindlers as well as an even greater number of well-meaning fanatics and incompetents have always found it possible to teach singing without the fear of exposure.

It has been suggested that voice teachers should be licensed, as are piano movers in some areas. The idea, logical as it seems on the surface, is unfortunately not feasible. Licensing a teacher implies checking by examination his knowledge of how to teach his subject; but knowledge of how to teach vocal technic cannot, as yet, be established by any known verbal means. A body of knowledge which possesses no standardized terminology cannot very well be made subject to examinations.

One could, of course, examine teachers of vocal technic in general musicianship, phonetics, languages, repertoire and such allied subjetcs. Vocal technic, however, is the only subject many if not most of such teachers admit to teaching.

Repertoire for instance is, as a rule, studied with pianists; languages and phonetics with a language teacher; musicianship with a theory teacher, either an instrumentalist or a composer; interpretation with a coach. Many so-called "voice specialists" do not even claim to know anything concerning music, languages or repertoire and declare that such matters have nothing to do with vocal technic, as conceived by them. We must admit, however, that even such a system of examination could not improve matters radically, for the ability to help a reasonably gifted student to develop an efficient manner of singing cannot, as yet, be checked quickly and easily by any known means at our disposal. Knowledge of a type which can be checked verbally has little to do with possession of such an ability.

I have known teachers of vocal technic who knew just barely enough of music, Italian, French and German and of repertoire to get along, yet they had an extraordinarily keen ear, a fine command of the metaphor, great psychological insight and were thus able to help their students. I have also known very learned men and women who knew a great deal about music, languages and repertoire who were hopeless as teachers of vocal technic. I have known great vocalists, fine artists who were justly famous for their singing, still they were unable to help a student overcome the simplest problems. I have also known people who never sang a note in their lives who could help vocal students to a degree one might not consider probable under the circumstances.

I do not believe that the situation as it exists now can be improved unless the student is made more conscious of what he wants from a teacher, of what he can expect the teacher to do for him and of what his own aims are. It obviously stands to reason that if the supply of students willing to support dishonest and incompetent teachers would diminish, the number of such teachers would diminish also. The fault lies not entirely with incompetent and dishonest teachers. It lies to a very considerable degree with the student who firmly believe that once he learns some "proper" and mysteriously efficient "trick" of directly, gymnastically controlling his muscles he will automatically become an efficient singer.

Of course, the student can not be made solely responsible for much of the ineffective and misleading teaching he unfortunately encounters so frequently. It is an indisputable fact that a number of very musically ungifted people who have little, if any, understanding of the complex coordinatory processes involved in singing, attempt to become professional singers and failing as such, they become teachers of vocal technic (which equals singing insofar as they and their students are concerned) simply because they are not able to earn their living as easily in any other way.

It is only natural for such might-have-been singers who never had any natural aptitude for music and for singing, to disregard completely the role that natural aptitude plays in any attempt to study singing, to distrust this natural aptitude and to be unwilling to recognize it when confronted with it.

It is only natural that, finding that the only way they themselves could ever manage to "sing" was mechanically by rote, they would insist in impressing such an attitude upon their students, talented or otherwise. It is only natural, for instance, for a singer who has a poor ear, or who has never used his ear, to be unfamiliar with the role it plays in the singing of a person who does happen to have a good ear. It is equally natural for such a singer to tell his students that it takes weeks of hard work to learn and memorize a song (since it does take weeks for him to do so) while it may take but thirty minutes for a student who happens to have a good ear and a good voice. It is only natural, too, for such a singer to instill a terrible fear in his students as to the immense complexity and difficulty of the process of learning how to sing.

When a talented person becomes influenced by such an attitude toward singing, he loses all confidence and courage as well as the joy of singing. As a result, he stops singing and begins to try to master vocal technic. Once this starts, he may never regain the ease and joy with which he sang in his ignorant days.

It seems to me that one of the most frequently encountered difficulties in the study and teaching of vocal technic is due to an insufficient realization of the fact that vocal technic (that is, an efficient manner of singing) cannot be developed successfully until the student possesses sufficient familiarity with his musical task as well as sufficient familiarity with his verbal task. One of the most unrealistic educational procedures ever evolved is the practice of trying to teach the student a manner of operating his vocal apparatus at the time when he knows neither the musical nor linguistic and phonetic aims which necessitate this operation, and is ignorant of the nature of the nonmuscular factors which govern and coordinate this operation. This procedure, which one very often encounters employed in the teaching of beginners is in my opinion responsible for most of the difficulties which the student encounters later.

A beginner must be taught how to employ his ear before he can be taught how to employ his voice. Teachers of vocal technic should be willing to teach elementary ear training, elementary phonetics and the rudiments of pronunciation in English, Italian, German and French for a year or so to their students practically to the exclusion of everything else. If they did so, they would eliminate the root of much of the tenseness in their student's singing which they so often try to reduce after so much has been done to create it. It does not seem, however, that such a procedure would meet with the general approval of teacher and student, primarily for economic reasons. It would seem, therefore, advisable to devise some preliminary procedure of study which could equip the student to occupy himself profitably with matters connected with evolving the most efficient manner of controlling his voice. Such a preliminary study could be summed up as follows:

1—Train your ear until you can learn music quickly and accurately either by first playing your part on some musical instrument and then singing it, or by reading it directly. Train your ear to the utmost. Consider it a major study. Do not attempt to study vocal technic until your musical ear is ready for it.

2—Train your speaking voice so that you can read and recite poetry sensibly, clearly and without tiring. Consider this a major study. Do not attempt to study vocal technic until your speech is ready for it.

3—Learn to pronounce in two languages—either Italian and German or Italian and French without singing in these languages.

4—Sing in any way you please as long as you make music and are comfortable, but only in your own language.

5—Do not try to improve your volume and range. Sing only things which seem comfortable to you. Do not attempt to go beyond your immediate capacity. Leave the development of your potentialities for later study.

6—Remember that reasonably comfortable singing only can form a basis for further improvement.

7—Remember that unless you can speak your words intelligently and without strain, you cannot attempt to sing them.

8—After you have managed to consolidate all these matters so that you can learn, memorize and sing acceptably
a simple song in English in, say, thirty minutes or an
hour, you may begin to think in terms of vocal technic.

By this time, you will have a fair idea of what you are
after and will be able to judge if the methods you employ
produce the desired results in your case or not.

I realize that this may be interpreted as a warning against
the study of vocal technic. It is not intended as such. Vocal
technic cannot, however, in my opinion, be developed effec-
tively by a student unless he knows enough about music,
speech and his own singing to be able to fulfill certain minimal
requirements on his own. Plunging into matters pertaining to
tone production before the matters which this tone production
is supposed to serve have been well assimilated, invariably
produces most undesirable effects even in the most talented
student.

VI. The Study of Repertoire

A vocal student who is considering the study of repertoire is confronted with a peculiar problem which practically no other performing musician seems to encounter in his repertoire studies. The very basic nature of each individual singer's instrument—his voice—must be constantly considered in relation to the music he wishes to perform. This is a consideration which most instrumentalists, perhaps excepting the organist, can easily disregard. The choice of a singer's repertoire (not taking into account his personal aesthetic preferences) is often determined not so much by the degree of skill with which he uses his voice, but by the basic physical nature of his individual voice.

This is not so where the instrumentalist is concerned. In his case, the determining factor (aside from personal preferences, of course) is the degree of skill with which he uses his instrument. The nature of his instrument is stable. Instruments are made to specifications, and the individual variations in each instrument are not sufficient to affect the basic nature of the type of sounds it is capable of producing when in good working order. By the type of sound I mean the pitch range, to some degree basic timbre and volume and to a lesser degree the quality of the timbre.

A good, fair or poor piano, for instance, naturally if in good working order, fulfills certain standard requirements of what a piano should be. Such requirements are fulfilled to a minimal degree even by a piano of the poorest manufacture. Thus a Beethoven concerto, for example, can be played on any make of pianoforte, provided it is in good working order. If a pianist cannot do so adequately, it means that *he* lacks the skill to do so. It does not mean that the instrument he is playing is incapable of fulfilling the demands made upon it by the music.

But a soprano who cannot adequately perform Isolde's "Liebestod," for instance, may: 1) lack the proper type of voice for this music and still be an excellent singer; 2) lack a mature enough voice to perform this music adequately at the time although possessing the proper type of voice and sufficient skill; 3) have both the type of mature voice necessary and the skill, but have certain individual imperfections in her voice as such which would prevent her from singing the piece adequately; and finally 4) lack the skill to do so.

The question whether such individual imperfections can or cannot be eradicated will have nothing to do with the fact that at the moment they prevent a singer from performing adequately some particular piece of music.

Each voice, as each instrument, has certain general limitations. One cannot play a low E, for instance, on a violin or a low A on a flute. One cannot expect the most excellent bass voice to produce an E above high C.

We classify voices into four main types primarily by the pitch range within which they operate: soprano, alto, tenor and bass. Within each type of voice, a number of subtypes can be found, characterized mainly by their timbre and the volume of sound a voice operating within such pitch range is able to produce. Thus we divide voices operating with the general soprano pitch range into many subtypes, such as coloratura soprano (with a fourth added to the normal so-

prano range), lyric coloratura, light lyric soprano, lyric soprano, spinto, dramatic soprano and so on.

However, within each of the subtypes we find voices possessing individual physical characteristics and limitations,
voices mature and immature, voices below or above certain
general specifications of the type.

Few students seem to realize that the inability to fulfill
the physical demands of some particular piece of vocal music
does not cast any reflection upon his skill and talent (as it
most certainly does in the case of an instrumentalist) since
such inability is often due to the basic structure of his vocal
apparatus, over which matter he, as a performer, has hardly
any control.

Besides, in some branches of vocal music such as opera,
operetta and musical comedy, the singer's appearance, physique and personality traits have to be taken into account as
well, since the ability to fulfill the purely vocal and musical
demands of the part is not, in itself, sufficient for a convincing
stage portrayal of a such a part. Compare the demands, for
instance, made upon a soprano's voice, physique and personality by the roles of Susanna (in Mozart's *The Marriage
of Figaro*), Leonora (in Verdi's *Il Trovatore*) and Brünn-
hilde (in Wagner's *Die Götterdämmerung*). All of this music
is written within practically the same pitch range. Yet each of
these three roles makes most dissimilar demands upon the
dynamic range, the timbre, the continuous use of some specific
part of the pitch range and upon the appearance, personality
and character of the singer. Normally, such contradictory
demands could not be successfully fulfilled by one person, no
matter how skillful and talented she were, if she did not possess a voice of an utterly extraordinary nature and an almost
protean personality.

Some authenticated examples of such an extraordinary

endowment can be found in the history of singing. The utterly extraordinary voice, however, capable of singing everything written within its pitch range is extremely rare, and one may be a most excellent singer without having such a voice.

One may be a most excellent singer and yet have a voice which is limited in volume and range. The fact that a singer may have a voice which does not happen to allow him to sing a high C of great beauty and power does not, in any way, disqualify him as a singer. It only disqualifies him as a singer of certain music or of certain types of music for which his individual voice is poorly suited. Thus the principle of type casting, whether one likes it or not, plays a most important part in most branches of vocal music, at least insofar as most singers are concerned.

It seems to me that many young singers are either unacquainted with this fact or choose to disregard it, fearing, perhaps, that by admitting the natural limitations of their voices of either temporary or permanent nature, they would also admit to the limitations of their skill in using them and to their degree of talent.

They seem to forget that the most excellent singers are those who are most keenly aware of the limitations of their voices, as well as of the nature of their personalities. Such a singer hardly ever ventures to appear before the public in the performance of a work which for some reason or another would draw the audience's attention to his vocal limitations or conflict with his personality.

There is nothing shameful in not being able to sing opera, or in not being able to sing a beautiful high C, though both, of course, are eminently desirable. One can become an excellent and most valuable soprano or tenor without ever having sung in public an operatic role or a high C. It depends on the talent one happens to have, on the basic quality of the voice, excepting the high C, on the skill with which one uses it and on the repertoire one chooses to sing. One may, however, easily nullify the labor of years and stunt an excellent talent by ill-advised and determined attempts at trying to convince the public that one has a voice of a different pitch range, different dynamic range and a different timbre than one naturally happens to have.

Vocal repertoire is so vast that practically every type of voice, even a voice to some degree limited and imperfect, can find enough excellent music which would not tax it beyond its natural capacity. A student trying to acquire a repertoire must try to realize where the strengths and the weaknesses of his voice are. He would do well to sing only such music which would allow him to employ his skill and talent without making impossible demands upon the physical nature of his individual vocal apparatus in its momentary state of development.

The most extraordinary demands made upon the dynamic range and the pitch range of a voice are to be found in the modern operatic repertoire, approximately from the time of Gluck to the present day. With few exceptions, all, even most of the secondary roles, in modern opera demand a pitch range of at least two octaves within which the singer is expected to operate freely. Again, with few exceptions, the volume demanded of all operatic voices is much above average since even the most lyric roles are supposed to be sung loudly enough to be heard over a good-sized orchestra in the uppermost balcony of a large opera house or theater. The most excellent singer whose voice cannot physically fulfill the demands of an operatic role cannot expect to succeed in opera as we know it today even though he may be able to sing operatic excerpts beautifully with pianoforte accompaniment in a medium-sized concert hall. The student should bear in mind that the so-called "very light operatic voices" are, insofar as their dynamic range is concerned, much beyond the capacity of what is considered an average "light voice."

As a general rule, students with an average vocal endowment ought not, in my opinion, busy themselves with operatic material. I should even venture to go further and to suggest that a student endowed with a very good but not an exceptional voice ought to wait until his voice becomes quite mature and until he learns to use it most skillfully before he begins to study opera seriously. I have seen too many young singers do themselves and their voices grave disservice by their insistence to study operatic roles which were simply physically beyond their reach either permanently or temporarily. Of course, a student can always find a few operatic excerpts which seem to suit his voice and not tax it beyond its physical capacity. Such exceptions seem in no way to nullify the general rule that operatic repertoire (excepting most of the seventeenth and eighteenth century operas) demands, most of the time, a physically exceptional, rather mature voice.

The principal reason why most modern opera demands voices of unusual range and power while most pre-nineteenth century opera demands only normal voices skillfully employed, is rather obvious. The more complex and musically independent the writing for the operatic orchestra began to be, the more brass and wood-wind instruments it employed, the more extreme the dramatic requirements of operatic roles began to grow the more taxing became the demands upon the physical properties of an operatic singer's voice.

Even a most cursory comparison between an operatic score by Pergolesi, Rameau or Handel, for instance, and an operatic score by Verdi or Wagner will disclose the extraordinary disparity in the acoustic demands made upon the singer in Pergolesi's time and in Wagner's time.

It is my contention that a student ought to concentrate first on learning how to sing music other than the nineteenth century opera. Concert repertoire, some oratorio and pre-nineteenth century opera offer an immense body of music written for the most part for voices of average pitch range and average dynamic range. Songs are seldom conceived by the composer to serve as display pieces for exhibiting extraordinary vocal endowment; operatic airs are very often conceived as such, especially in the nineteenth century grand opera. Pre-nineteenth century operatic airs, however, are very often conceived as display pieces for exhibiting the unusual skill in the use of one's voice.

An English-speaking student would do well to begin his repertoire studies with English songs and airs written before the nineteenth century. Dowland, Campion and other Elizabethan lutanists, Purcell and Handel, as well as innumerable minor composers of the latter half of the eighteenth century such as Dr. Arne, offer a wealth of music which seldom makes extraordinary demands upon a student's voice.

He could, at the same time, begin to study the songs of contemporary American and British composers, as well as folk songs, popular ballads and the so-called semiclassical songs. As he masters other languages, he could repeat this procedure, namely, the study of various styles of compositions, within one language group until he would have a fair knowledge of pre-nineteenth century, nineteenth century and contemporary vocal music of the English, German, French and Italian composers. Within each of such language groups, he could easily find a multitude of songs and airs suitable for just the type of voice he happens to have at the moment (provided, of course, he has at least an average voice) and not taxing it as such even though his voice may be, in several respects, limited and imperfect.

Insofar as the knowledge of vocal repertoire is concerned, many singers and students seem to lack musical curiosity to an extreme degree, and are thus often extremely ignorant of the wealth of music at their disposal and suitable for their voices. Because of this, they seem to believe that vocal repertoire consists mainly of famous display pieces of the type which singers with exceptional voices perform most of the time. This ignorance, as well as lack of the understanding of the problems involved in selecting suitable vocal repertoire often retards or even stunts the progress of many a student. The idea that unless a singer can sing grand opera he cannot be considered a singer, is unfortunately very prevalent among students. This idea has been responsible for many ruined voices and talents.

The idea, too, is sometimes encountered that every song must be sung in the key in which it happens to be printed instead of transposing it to suit the student's range. This idea has ruined many a fine song for many a talented student.

The choice of a student's repertoire should, in my opinion, be primarily based on the kind of voice he happens to have at the moment, and all the other factors should be taken into account only after this consideration had been given sufficient attention. I do not mean to imply that every student must be pigeonholed and unduly restricted in his choice of repertoire. I do believe that everyone should try to sing all types of music before making up his mind as to which type of vocal music will suit him best. Nevertheless, I utterly fail to see how a singer, and especially a young singer, can profit by insisting on struggling with music with which his voice as such seems to be unable to cope, or how a singer can expect the public to listen to a performance of this kind.

My advice to the student as well as to the young artist would be: when singing in public or preparing music to be sung in public, sing only the music which is kind to your voice. Only then will you be able to fulfill your obligations to the music, to the public and to yourself.

Standard repertoire, insofar as any individual songs and airs are concerned, seems hardly to exist in vocal music to the extent it does in instrumental music. However, there is a body of music written by certain composers which could be considered as standard. In other words, although one could not demand of every singer to be able to perform some particular songs of Schubert, for instance, every singer ought to be able to perform some songs of Schubert.

I shall endeavor here to give a very sketchy and inadequate list * of composers who are sufficiently important so that every competent singer is expected to have some of their music suitable to his voice in his repertoire (this list of composers excludes most of nineteenth century operatic composers):

ENGLISH Dowland, Campion and other Elizabethan lutanists.
Purcell
Handel
Dr. Arne and other eighteenth century composers.
Griffes, Vaughan Williams and other contemporary British and American composers.

ITALIAN Monteverdi and others of the Florentine school such as Peri and Caccini.
Scarlatti

* For an extended descriptive list of vocal repertoire, see *Music for the Voice* by Sergius Kagen, published by Rinehart & Company, Inc.

Pergolesi and other eighteenth century composers.
Respighi, Pizzetti, Santiliquido and other contemporary Italians.

FRENCH Lully
Rameau
Grétry and other eighteenth century composers such as Monsigny.
Gluck
Fauré
Duparc and other nineteenth century composers such as Chausson, Franck, etc.
Debussy and Ravel (not too suitable for certain types or voices).
Poulenc and other contemporary composers.

GERMAN Bach
Mozart
Haydn and Beethoven
Schubert
Schumann and other nineteenth century lied writers such as Mendelssohn, Franz, etc.
Brahms
Hugo Wolf
Strauss and other late nineteenth century and early twentieth century composers such Mahler, Marx, etc.

In addition, any English-speaking singer ought to know some songs of Moussorgsky, Tschaikowsky and Rachmaninoff, as well as some Scandinavian and Finnish songs (as for instance songs by Grieg and Kilpinen) in English translations.

A student who, for several years, searches the work of such composers for songs which appeal to him and which suit him vocally, cannot fail to build up an interesting, musically valid repertoire which he can perform. Such an exploration of vocal literature demands only musical curiosity, the ability to learn music adequately, the knowledge of one's limitations and industry.

I should venture to suggest that if the time which many a student spends on trying to conquer a few famous arias and songs which are beyond his physical capacities were spent in trying to find and to master music which he can reasonably hope to perform, he would not only learn to use his voice skillfully, but also would learn much music, most of which he could use for as long as he sings.

There is another facet of studying vocal repertoire which is very complex and of which I am reluctant to speak. It is commonly called interpretation. I shall discuss it only in a most limited manner. The reason which prompts me to discuss such a complex matter in this book is that apparently the whole concept of what an interpretation of a piece of vocal music may or should be is so vague in the minds of most students that it often prompts them to do most singular things to the music they perform and to themselves. My only aim in deciding to touch on this extremely difficult subject is to clarify some of the premises upon which a student's approach to interpretation may rest.

In my experience, I have come to the conclusion that many students seem to confuse interpretation with some form of distortion. Interpretation to many of them seems to mean a way of performing a song in so *individual* a manner that the identity of the performer could not possibly remain unnoticed even though the identity of the song itself may, because of this, become doubtful. It is, of course, nothing but an adolescent affectation, but it may become most obnoxious if it is left unchecked and allowed to become an integral part of one's way of singing.

The function of a musical performer is to allow the music to sound. Without him, the music which the composer has written remains nothing but a series of lines, dots and circles on ruled paper—lines, dots and circles that for all practical purposes are meaningless to most people. His job, therefore, is that of a middleman. He does not create music. He re-creates music—music which already exists in a very definite form but which, in that form, is beyond the reach of most people.

The fear that so many young performers seem to have of losing their individuality if they perform music accurately as the composer has set it down on paper, stems, of course, from the strong feeling of insecurity which is common among most young people. This fear is baseless. No two human beings can be alike (excepting, perhaps, identical twins), no two human beings can have voices which sound exactly alike, and no two human beings can perform a piece of vocal music alike no matter how hard they might try to do so.

Interpretation could, perhaps, be defined as one's individual reaction to the poem and the piece of music to which the poem has been set. Such reactions not only vary with each individual, but also *within* each individual, so that one can hardly perform a piece of vocal music twice in exactly the same way.

Interpretation of a song cannot and should not be standardized, but the text of a song (pitch, rhythm, words, grammar of the words, etc.) must, at all costs, be protected from every willful distortion. The idea that one cannot interpret a song without distorting its text is, in most cases, due to the fear of the performer that should he "do nothing to it" but sing it correctly, he will bore his public.

As I have said before, talent is undefinable. If one has talent, it will not be lost by performing music in the most accurate manner possible, and the public won't be bored. If one does not have talent, no amount of distortion will make a performance any more interesting. If one has talent, one cannot help but be deeply affected by the song one sings, especially if one likes the song and knows it well. The effect the song has upon the performer can, then, not be concealed from the public even if the performance of its text is most accurate. If one does not have talent, an inaccurate performance cannot be expected to serve as a substitute for strong and sincere feeling.

The principal reason I am discussing this subject is that so many students practically incapacitate themselves while singing by trying to force themselves to *feel* something they may not feel, by trying to convince the audience that they not only feel but feel deeply, by trying to draw attention to the way they sing, by trying to "put the song over" (which sometimes means grimacing and gesturing in most singular fashion) and by trying to make the music and the words "interesting"—which means mostly by making it unsteady in tempo, inaccurate as to grammar and, thus, phrasing, and even as to pitch and rhythm. The combination of all these regrettable and senseless activities often goes under the name of "interpretation."

As a rule, it accomplishes three things: it makes the public squirm in embarrassment; it makes the singer sing as inefficiently and as tensely as he possibly can; and it often distorts the poem and the music of a song beyond recognition.

I must again repeat that I do not believe that this book needs to discuss the very involved problems of interpretation in any comprehensive manner. Such a discussion would require a separate volume. The whole purpose of these few pages is to reassure the student that he won't lose his individuality as a singer if he sings accurately in time and on pitch and recites his words in a grammatically sensible fashion; to assure him that if he does not happen to feel anything too deeply while singing a song, he still can manage to give a very adequate performance of it by singing it as musically and efficiently as he knows how; and to convince him that planned mouthing, grimacing, gesturing and planned and calculated distortions of a song's text cannot serve as substitutes for an unconscious emotional compulsion which may prompt an almost involuntary gesture, a change of facial expression, an emphasis upon some word or some slight deviations from a metronomically precise rhythm.

Another purpose of this fully inadequate discussion is to warn the student of singing not to imitate the distortions of rhythm, tempo and phrasing which one sometimes encounters in the performances of singers possessing powerful, almost hypnotic stage personalities. Such distortions, if imitated without the inner drive of such artists, become nothing but ridiculous affectations. By imitating such distortions, one can no more reproduce the effect a powerful stage personality has upon the public than by imitating the dress, the walk or the coiffure of such a performer.

I believe that a student should never force himself to interpret. He would do well to let his imagination be kindled by the poem of a song, to let his musical feeling be affected by the music of it, and to try at all times to perform it as accurately and as vocally efficiently as he knows how without, of course, becoming petty or pedantic in his search for accuracy.

If he really has an interpretative talent, this talent will not only become disciplined in this fashion, but it will also develop. If he does not have such a talent, he will at least become an efficient singer. Nothing is quite so embarrassing and repulsive as an immature, inexperienced singer trying to pretend to be a daemonic interpreter, and making a spectacle of himself while ruining some masterpiece beyond recognition.

The singular idea which so many vocal students seem to have, that first one learns a song and then "puts feeling into it" makes a hollow mockery out of the word feeling. One can no more force oneself to feel a song than one can force oneself to feel the beauty of a sunset. The naive disrespect that so many young singers seem to have for their public is, of course, responsible for the idea that they can fool their listeners into believing that a song means more to the singer than it actually does. They ought to remember that musically untrained people are extraordinarily sensitive to genuine talent which, in the end, may be termed an ability to make others feel something one feels oneself.

Again I must warn those students who really feel their words and music very deeply not to allow this sincere feeling to become so undisciplined as to incapacitate them as performers. Once I watched a very gifted young soprano sing the second act of *Tosca*. When she came to her aria, she was so carried away by her emotions that she began to cry real tears. For a fraction of a second, the audience was deeply moved. What happened next was pitiful. She could not begin to sing her aria since she was sobbing. After a long and awkward pause, she finally forced herself to stop sobbing, but by that time, the tears had loosened one of her false eyelashes so that it hung across her cheek black and dangling. What followed was one of those things that one expects to see only in nightmares.

A performer must learn to reflect feeling. He cannot do so until he feels very deeply at some point or another during his study of a song or a role. Then he has to discipline this feeling so that he can reproduce it at will without being emotionally thrown off balance; he cannot substitute for it any number of mannerisms coupled with inaccuracies and expect the resulting "act" to affect his audience.

The whole problem of how to discipline and communicate one's emotions, of how to make them conform to the emotions which the composer wanted portrayed, of how to fuse one's own idea of the meaning of the poem with the idea which the composer had while setting it to music and with the stylistic requirements of each particular composer and the period to which his music belongs, is much too complex to be discussed here. The only reason I touched on this subject at all is to warn the student that by changing an eighth note into a sixteenth note while rolling his eyes, wringing his hands and making his voice quaver, he will not achieve anything insofar as the emotional impact of his singing is concerned.

VII. The Incompetent Professional and the Competent Amateur

It could be said that one of the most potent factors in preserving and expanding our musical culture is the part played in it by the intelligent and well-trained amateur. Equally, one of the most dangerous influences exercised upon our musical life of today could be attributed to the incompetent would-have-been or would-be professional. The amateur is perhaps the only free agent in our musical culture. No pressures can be brought to bear upon him insofar as his music making is concerned, since he makes music for his own pleasure only. Because of this he can, if he so wishes, acquaint himself with all types of music, and can thus help to mold the musical taste of the society in which he lives.

The amateur is the ultimate consumer of music of which the composer is the producer. The professional performer, being only a sort of a middleman in this relationship, is subject to a great number of pressures and can, as a rule, ill afford to perform any music which he believes may possibly alienate his public. Unless he is an utterly exceptional performer who is assured of a public no matter what he sings, or unless he performs for small, nonrepresentative groups of music lovers, he is forced to be very cautious and to sing mostly the "true and tried" favorites. This of course leads to a stagnating perpetuation of certain repertoire and affects our entire musical culture most adversely, since it virtually chokes off the supply of new music at its source.

The influence of well-informed, well-trained amateurs of the eighteenth and nineteenth centuries could be considered as one of the reasons (of course, by no means as the only reason) for the extraordinary expansion of musical culture during this period. The high artistic standards of these amateurs could be attributed, oddly enough, at least to some degree, to the fact that the calling of a professional musician was then as a rule in a very low estate socially. Because of this, only those utterly unable to resist the lure of devoting their lives to making music as well as those who had nothing to lose socially, would even dare to dream of braving all the disadvantages of being a professional musician in order to follow their inclination. Consequently, many a person who had the equipment as well as the training which could have enabled him to become a professional chose to remain an amateur and to contribute in this capacity to the musical life of his day.

Some hundred years ago, the calling of a professional singer seemed anything but honorable to all but the lowest economic and social strata of our society. Jenny Lind's managers, for instance, capitalized on the fact that although a professional singer she was not a "scarlet woman." Such curiosity was aroused by this circumstance that it completely overshadowed the quality of her singing insofar as a considerable part of her public was concerned. Many paid admission to see a singer reputed to be a lady, more than they did to hear her sing.

Where the average young people of good or middle-class families of the time were concerned, a study of singing was considered a most necessary accomplishment, but a study of singing for professional purposes was well-nigh unthinkable. Becoming a professional singer was tantamount to being disowned by one's family and friends; it meant social ostracism. At best, it meant more notoriety than fame. It could mean fame and fortune, but if it did, it was usually fame and fortune without social acceptance. In short, it meant a step of such magnitude that only very, very few even dared to contemplate it. Of course, there were exceptions. Famed and great singers did amass fortunes, did attain a grudgingly granted similitude of social equality with "their betters," but, generally speaking, no young lady or gentleman in his right mind ever thought seriously of sacrificing all for the sake of singing.

Compare this with the present day. A professional singer, if he is minimally successful, belongs to the very elite of our society. The opportunities are immense for earning enormous monetary rewards with just competent singing. A successful singer can, with luck, easily become very wealthy today, as well as attain a very high status in our social structure. No wonder that everyone who can carry a tune begins to think of singing in professional terms. What matters if his voice sounds rather unpleasant? It is only so because he has not studied. What matters if he cannot hear a difference between a major and a minor triad? It is only because he has not taken an ear training course. What matters if he cannot sing beyond one octave? It is so because he has no vocal technic.

Hitch your wagon to a star! All you need to attain fame, social prominence, money, honor and easy living for the rest of your life is to study for a few years with the "right" teacher and you will become a great singer! All you need is somebody to teach you *how* to become a great singer. And so it goes, day after day, and with the blessings and encouragement of parents, friends, Chambers of Commerce, scholarship funds, Rotarians, Elks, Odd Fellows, congressmen, senators, bankers, butchers and ministers of the gospel.

The field of professional singing is terribly overcrowded. Our musical life needs fewer inadequate professional singers and more intelligent amateurs. It needs above all more competent teachers of the kind who are not ungifted performers forced into teaching, or performers who had never thought of teaching seriously until they had to retire from the concert or operatic stage, but teachers who want to be teachers and who have trained themselves to be teachers even if they can perform. If only those who love it for its own sake would study singing, and if only those who have endowment and talent above average would think of becoming professional performers, much could be done to raise the general standard of our musical culture and singing.

Every student should ask himself the question, "Would you be willing to study singing if you knew that nothing would come out of it insofar as fame, money or profession goes?" and study only if he could honestly answer this question in the affirmative without reservation.

If he does study, he should try at all times to remember that there is no substitute for natural endowment or for talent, and that no method or manner of study which disregards this principle can be considered valid. He should hope for less but do more. He should not think in professional terms until he knows that he has the endowment and the talent to be a professional. He should never say, if I cannot be a successful singer, I can always teach! Teaching under such circumstances, he will unwittingly force himself to perpetuate his inadequacies and in turn may harm many a talented pupil. If he wants to teach, he must, first of all, want to teach for the love of teaching. Then he must make it his business to learn enough to be able to teach and to form an attitude toward teaching an art which is based on the recognition of the fact that no one can teach an ungifted person how to be less ungifted.

The teaching of singing is an honorable and rewarding profession, an art in itself and an exciting activity, but it is so only for those who do it willingly. The teaching of singing only because one did not have enough natural endowment for singing professionally, or only because it offers an opportunity to make ends meet, is a form of cruel, frustrating and deceitful parasitism.

No one can tell before he tries whether or not he can sing. Everyone who wants to should try, but after a few years of study, one can begin to think in terms of being an amateur, a performer or a teacher or both, for in a few years of intelligent study, one can easily take stock of one's capabilities.

If more young people would begin the study of singing for the sake of learning all that can be learned, and not for the sake of trying to learn how to be something they are not, they and the rest of us would all stand to gain immeasurably by such study.

A CATALOGUE OF SELECTED DOVER BOOKS
IN ALL FIELDS OF INTEREST

A CATALOGUE OF SELECTED DOVER BOOKS
IN ALL FIELDS OF INTEREST

AMERICA'S OLD MASTERS, James T. Flexner. Four men emerged unexpectedly from provincial 18th century America to leadership in European art: Benjamin West, J. S. Copley, C. R. Peale, Gilbert Stuart. Brilliant coverage of lives and contributions. Revised, 1967 edition. 69 plates. 365pp. of text.

21806-6 Paperbound $3.00

FIRST FLOWERS OF OUR WILDERNESS: AMERICAN PAINTING, THE COLONIAL PERIOD, James T. Flexner. Painters, and regional painting traditions from earliest Colonial times up to the emergence of Copley, West and Peale Sr., Foster, Gustavus Hesselius, Feke, John Smibert and many anonymous painters in the primitive manner. Engaging presentation, with 162 illustrations. xxii + 368pp.

22180-6 Paperbound $3.50

THE LIGHT OF DISTANT SKIES: AMERICAN PAINTING, 1760-1835, James T. Flexner. The great generation of early American painters goes to Europe to learn and to teach: West, Copley, Gilbert Stuart and others. Allston, Trumbull, Morse; also contemporary American painters—primitives, derivatives, academics—who remained in America. 102 illustrations. xiii + 306pp. 22179-2 Paperbound $3.00

A HISTORY OF THE RISE AND PROGRESS OF THE ARTS OF DESIGN IN THE UNITED STATES, William Dunlap. Much the richest mine of information on early American painters, sculptors, architects, engravers, miniaturists, etc. The only source of information for scores of artists, the major primary source for many others. Unabridged reprint of rare original 1834 edition, with new introduction by James T. Flexner, and 394 new illustrations. Edited by Rita Weiss. 6⅝ x 9⅝.

21695-0, 21696-9, 21697-7 Three volumes, Paperbound $13.50

EPOCHS OF CHINESE AND JAPANESE ART, Ernest F. Fenollosa. From primitive Chinese art to the 20th century, thorough history, explanation of every important art period and form, including Japanese woodcuts; main stress on China and Japan, but Tibet, Korea also included. Still unexcelled for its detailed, rich coverage of cultural background, aesthetic elements, diffusion studies, particularly of the historical period. 2nd, 1913 edition. 242 illustrations. lii + 439pp. of text.

20364-6, 20365-4 Two volumes, Paperbound $6.00

THE GENTLE ART OF MAKING ENEMIES, James A. M. Whistler. Greatest wit of his day deflates Oscar Wilde, Ruskin, Swinburne; strikes back at inane critics, exhibitions, art journalism; aesthetics of impressionist revolution in most striking form. Highly readable classic by great painter. Reproduction of edition designed by Whistler. Introduction by Alfred Werner. xxxvi + 334pp.

21875-9 Paperbound $2.50

VISUAL ILLUSIONS: THEIR CAUSES, CHARACTERISTICS, AND APPLICATIONS, Matthew Luckiesh. Thorough description and discussion of optical illusion, geometric and perspective, particularly; size and shape distortions, illusions of color, of motion; natural illusions; use of illusion in art and magic, industry, etc. Most useful today with op art, also for classical art. Scores of effects illustrated. Introduction by William H. Ittleson. 100 illustrations. xxi + 252pp.

21530-X Paperbound $2.00

A HANDBOOK OF ANATOMY FOR ART STUDENTS, Arthur Thomson. Thorough, virtually exhaustive coverage of skeletal structure, musculature, etc. Full text, supplemented by anatomical diagrams and drawings and by photographs of undraped figures. Unique in its comparison of male and female forms, pointing out differences of contour, texture, form. 211 figures, 40 drawings, 86 photographs. xx + 459pp. 5⅜ x 8⅜.

21163-0 Paperbound $3.50

150 MASTERPIECES OF DRAWING, Selected by Anthony Toney. Full page reproductions of drawings from the early 16th to the end of the 18th century, all beautifully reproduced: Rembrandt, Michelangelo, Dürer, Fragonard, Urs, Graf, Wouwerman, many others. First-rate browsing book, model book for artists. xviii + 150pp. 8⅜ x 11¼.

21032-4 Paperbound $2.50

THE LATER WORK OF AUBREY BEARDSLEY, Aubrey Beardsley. Exotic, erotic, ironic masterpieces in full maturity: Comedy Ballet, Venus and Tannhauser, Pierrot, Lysistrata, Rape of the Lock, Savoy material, Ali Baba, Volpone, etc. This material revolutionized the art world, and is still powerful, fresh, brilliant. With *The Early Work,* all Beardsley's finest work. 174 plates, 2 in color. xiv + 176pp. 8⅛ x 11.

21817-1 Paperbound $3.00

DRAWINGS OF REMBRANDT, Rembrandt van Rijn. Complete reproduction of fabulously rare edition by Lippmann and Hofstede de Groot, completely reedited, updated, improved by Prof. Seymour Slive, Fogg Museum. Portraits, Biblical sketches, landscapes, Oriental types, nudes, episodes from classical mythology—All Rembrandt's fertile genius. Also selection of drawings by his pupils and followers. "Stunning volumes," *Saturday Review.* 550 illustrations. lxxviii + 552pp. 9⅛ x 12¼.

21485-0, 21486-9 Two volumes, Paperbound $7.00

THE DISASTERS OF WAR, Francisco Goya. One of the masterpieces of Western civilization—83 etchings that record Goya's shattering, bitter reaction to the Napoleonic war that swept through Spain after the insurrection of 1808 and to war in general. Reprint of the first edition, with three additional plates from Boston's Museum of Fine Arts. All plates facsimile size. Introduction by Philip Hofer, Fogg Museum. v + 97pp. 9⅜ x 8¼.

21872-4 Paperbound $2.00

GRAPHIC WORKS OF ODILON REDON. Largest collection of Redon's graphic works ever assembled: 172 lithographs, 28 etchings and engravings, 9 drawings. These include some of his most famous works. All the plates from *Odilon Redon: oeuvre graphique complet,* plus additional plates. New introduction and caption translations by Alfred Werner. 209 illustrations. xxvii + 209pp. 9⅛ x 12¼.

21966-8 Paperbound $4.00

DESIGN BY ACCIDENT; A BOOK OF "ACCIDENTAL EFFECTS" FOR ARTISTS AND DESIGNERS, James F. O'Brien. Create your own unique, striking, imaginative effects by "controlled accident" interaction of materials: paints and lacquers, oil and water based paints, splatter, crackling materials, shatter, similar items. Everything you do will be different; first book on this limitless art, so useful to both fine artist and commercial artist. Full instructions. 192 plates showing "accidents," 8 in color. viii + 215pp. 8⅜ x 11¼. 21942-9 Paperbound $3.50

THE BOOK OF SIGNS, Rudolf Koch. Famed German type designer draws 493 beautiful symbols: religious, mystical, alchemical, imperial, property marks, runes, etc. Remarkable fusion of traditional and modern. Good for suggestions of timelessness, smartness, modernity. Text. vi + 104pp. 6⅛ x 9¼.
20162-7 Paperbound $1.25

HISTORY OF INDIAN AND INDONESIAN ART, Ananda K. Coomaraswamy. An unabridged republication of one of the finest books by a great scholar in Eastern art. Rich in descriptive material, history, social backgrounds; Sunga reliefs, Rajput paintings, Gupta temples, Burmese frescoes, textiles, jewelry, sculpture, etc. 400 photos. viii + 423pp. 6⅜ x 9¾. 21436-2 Paperbound $4.00

PRIMITIVE ART, Franz Boas. America's foremost anthropologist surveys textiles, ceramics, woodcarving, basketry, metalwork, etc.; patterns, technology, creation of symbols, style origins. All areas of world, but very full on Northwest Coast Indians. More than 350 illustrations of baskets, boxes, totem poles, weapons, etc. 378 pp.
20025-6 Paperbound $3.00

THE GENTLEMAN AND CABINET MAKER'S DIRECTOR, Thomas Chippendale. Full reprint (third edition, 1762) of most influential furniture book of all time, by master cabinetmaker. 200 plates, illustrating chairs, sofas, mirrors, tables, cabinets, plus 24 photographs of surviving pieces. Biographical introduction by N. Bienenstock. vi + 249pp. 9⅞ x 12¾. 21601-2 Paperbound $4.00

AMERICAN ANTIQUE FURNITURE, Edgar G. Miller, Jr. The basic coverage of all American furniture before 1840. Individual chapters cover type of furniture— clocks, tables, sideboards, etc.—chronologically, with inexhaustible wealth of data. More than 2100 photographs, all identified, commented on. Essential to all early American collectors. Introduction by H. E. Keyes. vi + 1106pp. 7⅞ x 10¾.
21599-7, 21600-4 Two volumes, Paperbound $10.00

PENNSYLVANIA DUTCH AMERICAN FOLK ART, Henry J. Kauffman. 279 photos, 28 drawings of tulipware, Fraktur script, painted tinware, toys, flowered furniture, quilts, samplers, hex signs, house interiors, etc. Full descriptive text. Excellent for tourist, rewarding for designer, collector. Map. 146pp. 7⅞ x 10¾.
21205-X Paperbound $2.50

EARLY NEW ENGLAND GRAVESTONE RUBBINGS, Edmund V. Gillon, Jr. 43 photographs, 226 carefully reproduced rubbings show heavily symbolic, sometimes macabre early gravestones, up to early 19th century. Remarkable early American primitive art, occasionally strikingly beautiful; always powerful. Text. xxvi + 207pp. 8⅜ x 11¼. 21380-3 Paperbound $3.50

ALPHABETS AND ORNAMENTS, Ernst Lehner. Well-known pictorial source for decorative alphabets, script examples, cartouches, frames, decorative title pages, calligraphic initials, borders, similar material. 14th to 19th century, mostly European. Useful in almost any graphic arts designing, varied styles. 750 illustrations. 256pp. 7 x 10. 21905-4 Paperbound $4.00

PAINTING: A CREATIVE APPROACH, Norman Colquhoun. For the beginner simple guide provides an instructive approach to painting: major stumbling blocks for beginner; overcoming them, technical points; paints and pigments; oil painting; watercolor and other media and color. New section on "plastic" paints. Glossary. Formerly *Paint Your Own Pictures*. 221pp. 22000-1 Paperbound $1.75

THE ENJOYMENT AND USE OF COLOR, Walter Sargent. Explanation of the relations between colors themselves and between colors in nature and art, including hundreds of little-known facts about color values, intensities, effects of high and low illumination, complementary colors. Many practical hints for painters, references to great masters. 7 color plates, 29 illustrations. x + 274pp.
20944-X Paperbound $2.50

THE NOTEBOOKS OF LEONARDO DA VINCI, compiled and edited by Jean Paul Richter. 1566 extracts from original manuscripts reveal the full range of Leonardo's versatile genius: all his writings on painting, sculpture, architecture, anatomy, astronomy, geography, topography, physiology, mining, music, etc., in both Italian and English, with 186 plates of manuscript pages and more than 500 additional drawings. Includes studies for the Last Supper, the lost Sforza monument, and other works. Total of xlvii + 866pp. 7⅞ x 10¾.
22572-0, 22573-9 Two volumes, Paperbound $10.00

MONTGOMERY WARD CATALOGUE OF 1895. Tea gowns, yards of flannel and pillow-case lace, stereoscopes, books of gospel hymns, the New Improved Singer Sewing Machine, side saddles, milk skimmers, straight-edged razors, high-button shoes, spittoons, and on and on . . . listing some 25,000 items, practically all illustrated. Essential to the shoppers of the 1890's, it is our truest record of the spirit of the period. Unaltered reprint of Issue No. 57, Spring and Summer 1895. Introduction by Boris Emmet. Innumerable illustrations. xiii + 624pp. 8½ x 11⅝.
22377-9 Paperbound $6.95

THE CRYSTAL PALACE EXHIBITION ILLUSTRATED CATALOGUE (LONDON, 1851). One of the wonders of the modern world—the Crystal Palace Exhibition in which all the nations of the civilized world exhibited their achievements in the arts and sciences—presented in an equally important illustrated catalogue. More than 1700 items pictured with accompanying text—ceramics, textiles, cast-iron work, carpets, pianos, sleds, razors, wall-papers, billiard tables, beehives, silverware and hundreds of other artifacts—represent the focal point of Victorian culture in the Western World. Probably the largest collection of Victorian decorative art ever assembled— indispensable for antiquarians and designers. Unabridged republication of the Art-Journal Catalogue of the Great Exhibition of 1851, with all terminal essays. New introduction by John Gloag, F.S.A. xxxiv + 426pp. 9 x 12.
22503-8 Paperbound $4.50

A HISTORY OF COSTUME, Carl Köhler. Definitive history, based on surviving pieces of clothing primarily, and paintings, statues, etc. secondarily. Highly readable text, supplemented by 594 illustrations of costumes of the ancient Mediterranean peoples, Greece and Rome, the Teutonic prehistoric period; costumes of the Middle Ages, Renaissance, Baroque, 18th and 19th centuries. Clear, measured patterns are provided for many clothing articles. Approach is practical throughout. Enlarged by Emma von Sichart. 464pp. 21030-8 Paperbound $3.50

ORIENTAL RUGS, ANTIQUE AND MODERN, Walter A. Hawley. A complete and authoritative treatise on the Oriental rug—where they are made, by whom and how, designs and symbols, characteristics in detail of the six major groups, how to distinguish them and how to buy them. Detailed technical data is provided on periods, weaves, warps, wefts, textures, sides, ends and knots, although no technical background is required for an understanding. 11 color plates, 80 halftones, 4 maps. vi + 320pp. 6⅛ x 9⅛. 22366-3 Paperbound $5.00

TEN BOOKS ON ARCHITECTURE, Vitruvius. By any standards the most important book on architecture ever written. Early Roman discussion of aesthetics of building, construction methods, orders, sites, and every other aspect of architecture has inspired, instructed architecture for about 2,000 years. Stands behind Palladio, Michelangelo, Bramante, Wren, countless others. Definitive Morris H. Morgan translation. 68 illustrations. xii + 331pp. 20645-9 Paperbound $2.50

THE FOUR BOOKS OF ARCHITECTURE, Andrea Palladio. Translated into every major Western European language in the two centuries following its publication in 1570, this has been one of the most influential books in the history of architecture. Complete reprint of the 1738 Isaac Ware edition. New introduction by Adolf Placzek, Columbia Univ. 216 plates. xxii + 110pp. of text. 9½ x 12¾. 21308-0 Clothbound $10.00

STICKS AND STONES: A STUDY OF AMERICAN ARCHITECTURE AND CIVILIZATION, Lewis Mumford.One of the great·classics of American cultural history. American architecture from the medieval-inspired earliest forms to the early 20th century; evolution of structure and style, and reciprocal influences on environment. 21 photographic illustrations. 238pp. 20202-X Paperbound $2.00

THE AMERICAN BUILDER'S COMPANION, Asher Benjamin. The most widely used early 19th century architectural style and source book, for colonial up into Greek Revival periods. Extensive development of geometry of carpentering, construction of sashes, frames, doors, stairs; plans and elevations of domestic and other buildings. Hundreds of thousands of houses were built according to this book, now invaluable to historians, architects, restorers, etc. 1827 edition. 59 plates. 114pp. 7⅞ x 10¾. 22236-5 Paperbound $3.00

DUTCH HOUSES IN THE HUDSON VALLEY BEFORE 1776, Helen Wilkinson Reynolds. The standard survey of the Dutch colonial house and outbuildings, with constructional features, decoration, and local history associated with individual homesteads. Introduction by Franklin D. Roosevelt. Map. 150 illustrations. 469pp. 6⅝ x 9¼. 21469-9 Paperbound $4.00

THE ARCHITECTURE OF COUNTRY HOUSES, Andrew J. Downing. Together with Vaux's *Villas and Cottages* this is the basic book for Hudson River Gothic architecture of the middle Victorian period. Full, sound discussions of general aspects of housing, architecture, style, decoration, furnishing, together with scores of detailed house plans, illustrations of specific buildings, accompanied by full text. Perhaps the most influential single American architectural book. 1850 edition. Introduction by J. Stewart Johnson. 321 figures, 34 architectural designs. xvi + 560pp.
22003-6 Paperbound $4.00

LOST EXAMPLES OF COLONIAL ARCHITECTURE, John Mead Howells. Full-page photographs of buildings that have disappeared or been so altered as to be denatured, including many designed by major early American architects. 245 plates. xvii + 248pp. 7⅞ x 10¾. 21143-6 Paperbound $3.50

DOMESTIC ARCHITECTURE OF THE AMERICAN COLONIES AND OF THE EARLY REPUBLIC, Fiske Kimball. Foremost architect and restorer of Williamsburg and Monticello covers nearly 200 homes between 1620-1825. Architectural details, construction, style features, special fixtures, floor plans, etc. Generally considered finest work in its area. 219 illustrations of houses, doorways, windows, capital mantels. xx + 314pp. 7⅞ x 10¾. 21743-4 Paperbound $4.00

EARLY AMERICAN ROOMS: 1650-1858, edited by Russell Hawes Kettell. Tour of 12 rooms, each representative of a different era in American history and each furnished, decorated, designed and occupied in the style of the era. 72 plans and elevations, 8-page color section, etc., show fabrics, wall papers, arrangements, etc. Full descriptive text. xvii + 200pp. of text. 8⅜ x 11¼.
21633-0 Paperbound $5.00

THE FITZWILLIAM VIRGINAL BOOK, edited by J. Fuller Maitland and W. B. Squire. Full modern printing of famous early 17th-century ms. volume of 300 works by Morley, Byrd, Bull, Gibbons, etc. For piano or other modern keyboard instrument; easy to read format. xxxvi + 938pp. 8⅜ x 11.
21068-5, 21069-3 Two volumes, Paperbound $10.00

KEYBOARD MUSIC, Johann Sebastian Bach. Bach Gesellschaft edition. A rich selection of Bach's masterpieces for the harpsichord: the six English Suites, six French Suites, the six Partitas (Clavierübung part I), the Goldberg Variations (Clavierübung part IV), the fifteen Two-Part Inventions and the fifteen Three-Part Sinfonias. Clearly reproduced on large sheets with ample margins; eminently playable. vi + 312pp. 8⅛ x 11. 22360-4 Paperbound $5.00

THE MUSIC OF BACH: AN INTRODUCTION, Charles Sanford Terry. A fine, nontechnical introduction to Bach's music, both instrumental and vocal. Covers organ music, chamber music, passion music, other types. Analyzes themes, developments, innovations. x + 114pp. 21075-8 Paperbound $1.25

BEETHOVEN AND HIS NINE SYMPHONIES, Sir George Grove. Noted British musicologist provides best history, analysis, commentary on symphonies. Very thorough, rigorously accurate; necessary to both advanced student and amateur music lover. 436 musical passages. vii + 407 pp. 20334-4 Paperbound $2.50

JOHANN SEBASTIAN BACH, Philipp Spitta. One of the great classics of musicology, this definitive analysis of Bach's music (and life) has never been surpassed. Lucid, nontechnical analyses of hundreds of pieces (30 pages devoted to St. Matthew Passion, 26 to B Minor Mass). Also includes major analysis of 18th-century music. 450 musical examples. 40-page musical supplement. Total of xx + 1799pp.

(EUK) 22278-0, 22279-9 Two volumes, Clothbound $15.00

MOZART AND HIS PIANO CONCERTOS, Cuthbert Girdlestone. The only full-length study of an important area of Mozart's creativity. Provides detailed analyses of all 23 concertos, traces inspirational sources. 417 musical examples. Second edition. 509pp.

(USO) 21271-8 Paperbound $3.50

THE PERFECT WAGNERITE: A COMMENTARY ON THE NIBLUNG'S RING, George Bernard Shaw. Brilliant and still relevant criticism in remarkable essays on Wagner's Ring cycle, Shaw's ideas on political and social ideology behind the plots, role of Leitmotifs, vocal requisites, etc. Prefaces. xxi + 136pp.

21707-8 Paperbound $1.50

DON GIOVANNI, W. A. Mozart. Complete libretto, modern English translation; biographies of composer and librettist; accounts of early performances and critical reaction. Lavishly illustrated. All the material you need to understand and appreciate this great work. Dover Opera Guide and Libretto Series; translated and introduced by Ellen Bleiler. 92 illustrations. 209pp.

21134-7 Paperbound $1.50

HIGH FIDELITY SYSTEMS: A LAYMAN'S GUIDE, Roy F. Allison. All the basic information you need for setting up your own audio system: high fidelity and stereo record players, tape records, F.M. Connections, adjusting tone arm, cartridge, checking needle alignment, positioning speakers, phasing speakers, adjusting hums, trouble-shooting, maintenance, and similar topics. Enlarged 1965 edition. More than 50 charts, diagrams, photos. iv + 91pp.

21514-8 Paperbound $1.25

REPRODUCTION OF SOUND, Edgar Villchur. Thorough coverage for laymen of high fidelity systems, reproducing systems in general, needles, amplifiers, preamps, loudspeakers, feedback, explaining physical background. "A rare talent for making technicalities vividly comprehensible," R. Darrell, *High Fidelity*. 69 figures. iv + 92pp.

21515-6 Paperbound $1.00

HEAR ME TALKIN' TO YA: THE STORY OF JAZZ AS TOLD BY THE MEN WHO MADE IT, Nat Shapiro and Nat Hentoff. Louis Armstrong, Fats Waller, Jo Jones, Clarence Williams, Billy Holiday, Duke Ellington, Jelly Roll Morton and dozens of other jazz greats tell how it was in Chicago's South Side, New Orleans, depression Harlem and the modern West Coast as jazz was born and grew. xvi + 429pp.

21726-4 Paperbound $2.50

FABLES OF AESOP, translated by Sir Roger L'Estrange. A reproduction of the very rare 1931 Paris edition; a selection of the most interesting fables, together with 50 imaginative drawings by Alexander Calder. v + 128pp. 6½x9¼.

21780-9 Paperbound $1.50

AGAINST THE GRAIN (A REBOURS), Joris K. Huysmans. Filled with weird images, evidences of a bizarre imagination, exotic experiments with hallucinatory drugs, rich tastes and smells and the diversions of its sybarite hero Duc Jean des Esseintes, this classic novel pushed 19th-century literary decadence to its limits. Full unabridged edition. Do not confuse this with abridged editions generally sold. Introduction by Havelock Ellis. xlix + 206pp. 22190-3 Paperbound $2.00

VARIORUM SHAKESPEARE: HAMLET. Edited by Horace H. Furness; a landmark of American scholarship. Exhaustive footnotes and appendices treat all doubtful words and phrases, as well as suggested critical emendations throughout the play's history. First volume contains editor's own text, collated with all Quartos and Folios. Second volume contains full first Quarto, translations of Shakespeare's sources (Belleforest, and Saxo Grammaticus), Der Bestrafte Brudermord, and many essays on critical and historical points of interest by major authorities of past and present. Includes details of staging and costuming over the years. By far the best edition available for serious students of Shakespeare. Total of xx + 905pp. 21004-9, 21005-7, 2 volumes, Paperbound $5.50

A LIFE OF WILLIAM SHAKESPEARE, Sir Sidney Lee. This is the standard life of Shakespeare, summarizing everything known about Shakespeare and his plays. Incredibly rich in material, broad in coverage, clear and judicious, it has served thousands as the best introduction to Shakespeare. 1931 edition. 9 plates. xxix + 792pp. (USO) 21967-4 Paperbound $3.75

MASTERS OF THE DRAMA, John Gassner. Most comprehensive history of the drama in print, covering every tradition from Greeks to modern Europe and America, including India, Far East, etc. Covers more than 800 dramatists, 2000 plays, with biographical material, plot summaries, theatre history, criticism, etc. "Best of its kind in English," New Republic. 77 illustrations. xxii + 890pp. 20100-7 Clothbound $8.50

THE EVOLUTION OF THE ENGLISH LANGUAGE, George McKnight. The growth of English, from the 14th century to the present. Unusual, non-technical account presents basic information in very interesting form: sound shifts, change in grammar and syntax, vocabulary growth, similar topics. Abundantly illustrated with quotations. Formerly Modern English in the Making. xii + 590pp. 21932-1 Paperbound $3.50

AN ETYMOLOGICAL DICTIONARY OF MODERN ENGLISH, Ernest Weekley. Fullest, richest work of its sort, by foremost British lexicographer. Detailed word histories, including many colloquial and archaic words; extensive quotations. Do not confuse this with the Concise Etymological Dictionary, which is much abridged. Total of xxvii + 830pp. 6½ x 9¼. 21873-2, 21874-0 Two volumes, Paperbound $6.00

FLATLAND: A ROMANCE OF MANY DIMENSIONS, E. A. Abbott. Classic of science-fiction explores ramifications of life in a two-dimensional world, and what happens when a three-dimensional being intrudes. Amusing reading, but also useful as introduction to thought about hyperspace. Introduction by Banesh Hoffmann. 16 illustrations. xx + 103pp. 20001-9 Paperbound $1.00

POEMS OF ANNE BRADSTREET, edited with an introduction by Robert Hutchinson. A new selection of poems by America's first poet and perhaps the first significant woman poet in the English language. 48 poems display her development in works of considerable variety—love poems, domestic poems, religious meditations, formal elegies, "quaternions," etc. Notes, bibliography. viii + 222pp.
22160-1 Paperbound $2.00

THREE GOTHIC NOVELS: THE CASTLE OF OTRANTO BY HORACE WALPOLE; VATHEK BY WILLIAM BECKFORD; THE VAMPYRE BY JOHN POLIDORI, WITH FRAGMENT OF A NOVEL BY LORD BYRON, edited by E. F. Bleiler. The first Gothic novel, by Walpole; the finest Oriental tale in English, by Beckford; powerful Romantic supernatural story in versions by Polidori and Byron. All extremely important in history of literature; all still exciting, packed with supernatural thrills, ghosts, haunted castles, magic, etc. xl + 291pp.
21232-7 Paperbound $2.00

THE BEST TALES OF HOFFMANN, E. T. A. Hoffmann. 10 of Hoffmann's most important stories, in modern re-editings of standard translations: Nutcracker and the King of Mice, Signor Formica, Automata, The Sandman, Rath Krespel, The Golden Flowerpot, Master Martin the Cooper, The Mines of Falun, The King's Betrothed, A New Year's Eve Adventure. 7 illustrations by Hoffmann. Edited by E. F. Bleiler. xxxix + 419pp.
21793-0 Paperbound $2.50

GHOST AND HORROR STORIES OF AMBROSE BIERCE, Ambrose Bierce. 23 strikingly modern stories of the horrors latent in the human mind: The Eyes of the Panther, The Damned Thing, An Occurrence at Owl Creek Bridge, An Inhabitant of Carcosa, etc., plus the dream-essay, Visions of the Night. Edited by E. F. Bleiler. xxii + 199pp.
20767-6 Paperbound $1.50

BEST GHOST STORIES OF J. S. LeFANU, J. Sheridan LeFanu. Finest stories by Victorian master often considered greatest supernatural writer of all. Carmilla, Green Tea, The Haunted Baronet, The Familiar, and 12 others. Most never before available in the U. S. A. Edited by E. F. Bleiler. 8 illustrations from Victorian publications. xvii + 467pp.
20415-4 Paperbound $3.00

THE TIME STREAM, THE GREATEST ADVENTURE, AND THE PURPLE SAPPHIRE—THREE SCIENCE FICTION NOVELS, John Taine (Eric Temple Bell). Great American mathematician was also foremost science fiction novelist of the 1920's. *The Time Stream,* one of all-time classics, uses concepts of circular time; *The Greatest Adventure,* incredibly ancient biological experiments from Antarctica threaten to escape; The *Purple Sapphire,* superscience, lost races in Central Tibet, survivors of the Great Race. 4 illustrations by Frank R. Paul. v + 532pp.
21180-0 Paperbound $3.00

SEVEN SCIENCE FICTION NOVELS, H. G. Wells. The standard collection of the great novels. Complete, unabridged. *First Men in the Moon, Island of Dr. Moreau, War of the Worlds, Food of the Gods, Invisible Man, Time Machine, In the Days of the Comet.* Not only science fiction fans, but every educated person owes it to himself to read these novels. 1015pp.
20264-X Clothbound $5.00

LAST AND FIRST MEN AND STAR MAKER, TWO SCIENCE FICTION NOVELS, Olaf Stapledon. Greatest future histories in science fiction. In the first, human intelligence is the "hero," through strange paths of evolution, interplanetary invasions, incredible technologies, near extinctions and reemergences. Star Maker describes the quest of a band of star rovers for intelligence itself, through time and space: weird inhuman civilizations, crustacean minds, symbiotic worlds, etc. Complete, unabridged. v + 438pp. 21962-3 Paperbound $2.50

THREE PROPHETIC NOVELS, H. G. WELLS. Stages of a consistently planned future for mankind. *When the Sleeper Wakes,* and *A Story of the Days to Come,* anticipate *Brave New World* and *1984,* in the 21st Century; *The Time Machine,* only complete version in print, shows farther future and the end of mankind. All show Wells's greatest gifts as storyteller and novelist. Edited by E. F. Bleiler. x + 335pp. (USO) 20605-X Paperbound $2.25

THE DEVIL'S DICTIONARY, Ambrose Bierce. America's own Oscar Wilde—Ambrose Bierce—offers his barbed iconoclastic wisdom in over 1,000 definitions hailed by H. L. Mencken as "some of the most gorgeous witticisms in the English language." 145pp. 20487-1 Paperbound $1.25

MAX AND MORITZ, Wilhelm Busch. Great children's classic, father of comic strip, of two bad boys, Max and Moritz. Also Ker and Plunk (Plisch und Plumm), Cat and Mouse, Deceitful Henry, Ice-Peter, The Boy and the Pipe, and five other pieces. Original German, with English translation. Edited by H. Arthur Klein; translations by various hands and H. Arthur Klein. vi + 216pp. 20181-3 Paperbound $1.50

PIGS IS PIGS AND OTHER FAVORITES, Ellis Parker Butler. The title story is one of the best humor short stories, as Mike Flannery obfuscates biology and English. Also included, That Pup of Murchison's, The Great American Pie Company, and Perkins of Portland. 14 illustrations. v + 109pp. 21532-6 Paperbound $1.00

THE PETERKIN PAPERS, Lucretia P. Hale. It takes genius to be as stupidly mad as the Peterkins, as they decide to become wise, celebrate the "Fourth," keep a cow, and otherwise strain the resources of the Lady from Philadelphia. Basic book of American humor. 153 illustrations. 219pp. 20794-3 Paperbound $1.50

PERRAULT'S FAIRY TALES, translated by A. E. Johnson and S. R. Littlewood, with 34 full-page illustrations by Gustave Doré. All the original Perrault stories—Cinderella, Sleeping Beauty, Bluebeard, Little Red Riding Hood, Puss in Boots, Tom Thumb, etc.—with their witty verse morals and the magnificent illustrations of Doré. One of the five or six great books of European fairy tales. viii + 117pp. 8⅛ x 11. 22311-6 Paperbound $2.00

OLD HUNGARIAN FAIRY TALES, Baroness Orczy. Favorites translated and adapted by author of the *Scarlet Pimpernel.* Eight fairy tales include "The Suitors of Princess Fire-Fly," "The Twin Hunchbacks," "Mr. Cuttlefish's Love Story," and "The Enchanted Cat." This little volume of magic and adventure will captivate children as it has for generations. 90 drawings by Montagu Barstow. 96pp. (USO) 22293-4 Paperbound $1.95

THE RED FAIRY BOOK, Andrew Lang. Lang's color fairy books have long been children's favorites. This volume includes Rapunzel, Jack and the Bean-stalk and 35 other stories, familiar and unfamiliar. 4 plates, 93 illustrations x + 367pp.
21673-X Paperbound $2.00

THE BLUE FAIRY BOOK, Andrew Lang. Lang's tales come from all countries and all times. Here are 37 tales from Grimm, the Arabian Nights, Greek Mythology, and other fascinating sources. 8 plates, 130 illustrations. xi + 390pp.
21437-0 Paperbound $1.95

HOUSEHOLD STORIES BY THE BROTHERS GRIMM. Classic English-language edition of the well-known tales — Rumpelstiltskin, Snow White, Hansel and Gretel, The Twelve Brothers, Faithful John, Rapunzel, Tom Thumb (52 stories in all). Translated into simple, straightforward English by Lucy Crane. Ornamented with headpieces, vignettes, elaborate decorative initials and a dozen full-page illustrations by Walter Crane. x + 269pp.
21080-4 Paperbound $2.00

THE MERRY ADVENTURES OF ROBIN HOOD, Howard Pyle. The finest modern versions of the traditional ballads and tales about the great English outlaw. Howard Pyle's complete prose version, with every word, every illustration of the first edition. Do not confuse this facsimile of the original (1883) with modern editions that change text or illustrations. 23 plates plus many page decorations. xxii + 296pp.
22043-5 Paperbound $2.50

THE STORY OF KING ARTHUR AND HIS KNIGHTS, Howard Pyle. The finest children's version of the life of King Arthur; brilliantly retold by Pyle, with 48 of his most imaginative illustrations. xviii + 313pp. 6⅛ x 9¼.
21445-1 Paperbound $2.50

THE WONDERFUL WIZARD OF OZ, L. Frank Baum. America's finest children's book in facsimile of first edition with all Denslow illustrations in full color. The edition a child should have. Introduction by Martin Gardner. 23 color plates, scores of drawings. iv + 267pp.
20691-2 Paperbound $2.25

THE MARVELOUS LAND OF OZ, L. Frank Baum. The second Oz book, every bit as imaginative as the Wizard. The hero is a boy named Tip, but the Scarecrow and the Tin Woodman are back, as is the Oz magic. 16 color plates, 120 drawings by John R. Neill. 287pp.
20692-0 Paperbound $2.50

THE MAGICAL MONARCH OF MO, L. Frank Baum. Remarkable adventures in a land even stranger than Oz. The best of Baum's books not in the Oz series. 15 color plates and dozens of drawings by Frank Verbeck. xviii + 237pp.
21892-9 Paperbound $2.00

THE BAD CHILD'S BOOK OF BEASTS, MORE BEASTS FOR WORSE CHILDREN, A MORAL ALPHABET, Hilaire Belloc. Three complete humor classics in one volume. Be kind to the frog, and do not call him names . . . and 28 other whimsical animals. Familiar favorites and some not so well known. Illustrated by Basil Blackwell. 156pp.
(USO) 20749-8 Paperbound $1.25

EAST O' THE SUN AND WEST O' THE MOON, George W. Dasent. Considered the best of all translations of these Norwegian folk tales, this collection has been enjoyed by generations of children (and folklorists too). Includes True and Untrue, Why the Sea is Salt, East O' the Sun and West O' the Moon, Why the Bear is Stumpy-Tailed, Boots and the Troll, The Cock and the Hen, Rich Peter the Pedlar, and 52 more. The only edition with all 59 tales. 77 illustrations by Erik Werenskiold and Theodor Kittelsen. xv + 418pp. 22521-6 Paperbound $3.00

GOOPS AND HOW TO BE THEM, Gelett Burgess. Classic of tongue-in-cheek humor, masquerading as etiquette book. 87 verses, twice as many cartoons, show mischievous Goops as they demonstrate to children virtues of table manners, neatness, courtesy, etc. Favorite for generations. viii + 88pp. 6½ x 9¼.
22233-0 Paperbound $1.25

ALICE'S ADVENTURES UNDER GROUND, Lewis Carroll. The first version, quite different from the final *Alice in Wonderland,* printed out by Carroll himself with his own illustrations. Complete facsimile of the "million dollar" manuscript Carroll gave to Alice Liddell in 1864. Introduction by Martin Gardner. viii + 96pp. Title and dedication pages in color. 21482-6 Paperbound $1.25

THE BROWNIES, THEIR BOOK, Palmer Cox. Small as mice, cunning as foxes, exuberant and full of mischief, the Brownies go to the zoo, toy shop, seashore, circus, etc., in 24 verse adventures and 266 illustrations. Long a favorite, since their first appearance in St. Nicholas Magazine. xi + 144pp. 6⅝ x 9¼.
21265-3 Paperbound $1.75

SONGS OF CHILDHOOD, Walter De La Mare. Published (under the pseudonym Walter Ramal) when De La Mare was only 29, this charming collection has long been a favorite children's book. A facsimile of the first edition in paper, the 47 poems capture the simplicity of the nursery rhyme and the ballad, including such lyrics as I Met Eve, Tartary, The Silver Penny. vii + 106pp. 21972-0 Paperbound $1.25

THE COMPLETE NONSENSE OF EDWARD LEAR, Edward Lear. The finest 19th-century humorist-cartoonist in full: all nonsense limericks, zany alphabets, Owl and Pussycat, songs, nonsense botany, and more than 500 illustrations by Lear himself. Edited by Holbrook Jackson. xxix + 287pp. (USO) 20167-8 Paperbound $2.00

BILLY WHISKERS: THE AUTOBIOGRAPHY OF A GOAT, Frances Trego Montgomery. A favorite of children since the early 20th century, here are the escapades of that rambunctious, irresistible and mischievous goat—Billy Whiskers. Much in the spirit of *Peck's Bad Boy,* this is a book that children never tire of reading or hearing. All the original familiar illustrations by W. H. Fry are included: 6 color plates, 18 black and white drawings. 159pp. 22345-0 Paperbound $2.00

MOTHER GOOSE MELODIES. Faithful republication of the fabulously rare Munroe and Francis "copyright 1833" Boston edition—the most important Mother Goose collection, usually referred to as the "original." Familiar rhymes plus many rare ones, with wonderful old woodcut illustrations. Edited by E. F. Bleiler. 128pp. 4½ x 6⅜. 22577-1 Paperbound $1.25

TWO LITTLE SAVAGES; BEING THE ADVENTURES OF TWO BOYS WHO LIVED AS INDIANS AND WHAT THEY LEARNED, Ernest Thompson Seton. Great classic of nature and boyhood provides a vast range of woodlore in most palatable form, a genuinely entertaining story. Two farm boys build a teepee in woods and live in it for a month, working out Indian solutions to living problems, star lore, birds and animals, plants, etc. 293 illustrations. vii + 286pp.

20985-7 Paperbound $2.50

PETER PIPER'S PRACTICAL PRINCIPLES OF PLAIN & PERFECT PRONUNCIATION. Alliterative jingles and tongue-twisters of surprising charm, that made their first appearance in America about 1830. Republished in full with the spirited woodcut illustrations from this earliest American edition. 32pp. $4\frac{1}{2}$ x $6\frac{3}{8}$.

22560-7 Paperbound $1.00

SCIENCE EXPERIMENTS AND AMUSEMENTS FOR CHILDREN, Charles Vivian. 73 easy experiments, requiring only materials found at home or easily available, such as candles, coins, steel wool, etc.; illustrate basic phenomena like vacuum, simple chemical reaction, etc. All safe. Modern, well-planned. Formerly *Science Games for Children*. 102 photos, numerous drawings. 96pp. $6\frac{1}{8}$ x $9\frac{1}{4}$.

21856-2 Paperbound $1.25

AN INTRODUCTION TO CHESS MOVES AND TACTICS SIMPLY EXPLAINED, Leonard Barden. Informal intermediate introduction, quite strong in explaining reasons for moves. Covers basic material, tactics, important openings, traps, positional play in middle game, end game. Attempts to isolate patterns and recurrent configurations. Formerly *Chess*. 58 figures. 102pp. (USO) 21210-6 Paperbound $1.25

LASKER'S MANUAL OF CHESS, Dr. Emanuel Lasker. Lasker was not only one of the five great World Champions, he was also one of the ablest expositors, theorists, and analysts. In many ways, his Manual, permeated with his philosophy of battle, filled with keen insights, is one of the greatest works ever written on chess. Filled with analyzed games by the great players. A single-volume library that will profit almost any chess player, beginner or master. 308 diagrams. xli x 349pp.

20640-8 Paperbound $2.50

THE MASTER BOOK OF MATHEMATICAL RECREATIONS, Fred Schuh. In opinion of many the finest work ever prepared on mathematical puzzles, stunts, recreations; exhaustively thorough explanations of mathematics involved, analysis of effects, citation of puzzles and games. Mathematics involved is elementary. Translated by F. Göbel. 194 figures. xxiv + 430pp.

22134-2 Paperbound $3.00

MATHEMATICS, MAGIC AND MYSTERY, Martin Gardner. Puzzle editor for Scientific American explains mathematics behind various mystifying tricks: card tricks, stage "mind reading," coin and match tricks, counting out games, geometric dissections, etc. Probability sets, theory of numbers clearly explained. Also provides more than 400 tricks, guaranteed to work, that you can do. 135 illustrations. xii + 176pp.

20338-2 Paperbound $1.50

MATHEMATICAL PUZZLES FOR BEGINNERS AND ENTHUSIASTS, Geoffrey Mott-Smith. 189 puzzles from easy to difficult—involving arithmetic, logic, algebra, properties of digits, probability, etc.—for enjoyment and mental stimulus. Explanation of mathematical principles behind the puzzles. 135 illustrations. viii + 248pp.

20198-8 Paperbound $1.75

PAPER FOLDING FOR BEGINNERS, William D. Murray and Francis J. Rigney. Easiest book on the market, clearest instructions on making interesting, beautiful origami. Sail boats, cups, roosters, frogs that move legs, bonbon boxes, standing birds, etc. 40 projects; more than 275 diagrams and photographs. 94pp.

20713-7 Paperbound $1.00

TRICKS AND GAMES ON THE POOL TABLE, Fred Herrmann. 79 tricks and games— some solitaires, some for two or more players, some competitive games—to entertain you between formal games. Mystifying shots and throws, unusual caroms, tricks involving such props as cork, coins, a hat, etc. Formerly *Fun on the Pool Table*. 77 figures. 95pp.

21814-7 Paperbound $1.00

HAND SHADOWS TO BE THROWN UPON THE WALL: A SERIES OF NOVEL AND AMUSING FIGURES FORMED BY THE HAND, Henry Bursill. Delightful picturebook from great-grandfather's day shows how to make 18 different hand shadows: a bird that flies, duck that quacks, dog that wags his tail, camel, goose, deer, boy, turtle, etc. Only book of its sort. vi + 33pp. 6½ x 9¼.   21779-5 Paperbound $1.00

WHITTLING AND WOODCARVING, E. J. Tangerman. 18th printing of best book on market. "If you can cut a potato you can carve" toys and puzzles, chains, chessmen, caricatures, masks, frames, woodcut blocks, surface patterns, much more. Information on tools, woods, techniques. Also goes into serious wood sculpture from Middle Ages to present, East and West. 464 photos, figures. x + 293pp.

20965-2 Paperbound $2.00

HISTORY OF PHILOSOPHY, Julián Marias. Possibly the clearest, most easily followed, best planned, most useful one-volume history of philosophy on the market; neither skimpy nor overfull. Full details on system of every major philosopher and dozens of less important thinkers from pre-Socratics up to Existentialism and later. Strong on many European figures usually omitted. Has gone through dozens of editions in Europe. 1966 edition, translated by Stanley Appelbaum and Clarence Strowbridge. xviii + 505pp.

21739-6 Paperbound $3.00

YOGA: A SCIENTIFIC EVALUATION, Kovoor T. Behanan. Scientific but non-technical study of physiological results of yoga exercises; done under auspices of Yale U. Relations to Indian thought, to psychoanalysis, etc. 16 photos. xxiii + 270pp.

20505-3 Paperbound $2.50